CAMELS AND CROCS
ADVENTURES IN OUTBACK AUSTRALIA

CAMELS AND CROCS
ADVENTURES IN OUTBACK AUSTRALIA

MAGGIE RAMSAY

Copyright © 2020 by Maggie Ramsay
All Rights Reserved

No part of this book may be reproduced, stored in retrieval systems, or transmitted by any means, electronic, mechanical, photocopying, recorded or otherwise without written permission from the author.

Book design by Maureen Cutajar
Cover design by Jeanine Henning

ISBN: 978-0-6488893-0-4 (paperback)
ISBN: 978-0-6488893-1-1 (hardback)
ISBN: 978-0-6488893-2-8 (e-book)

DISCLAIMER

This is not intended to be a guidebook; it is my personal story of our travels in Outback Australia. Distances are in some instances approximate. Locations of places on the map are indicative only.

Apart from historical or geographical facts, the comments and descriptions of people and places in this book are solely the author's personal opinion.

Travel in remote Australia can be hazardous and should be approached with appropriate safety precautions and detailed planning.

*To my daughters Sibylla, Jessica and Zoe,
stars of most of the adventures in the other part of my life.*

ABOUT THE LANGUAGE

We speak English in Australia (which sometimes surprises people). We are mostly easy to understand, despite our funny accent, but we love slang and abbreviations and we have some unique words, so I have included a glossary at the end of the book.

I have used Australian spelling and units of measurement.

ACKNOWLEDGEMENTS

Our friends Nonie and Stuart have tackled many remote places and fearsome tracks with us and are unfailingly brave and resourceful. On part of this trip we were joined by Merren and Arthur who were also intrepid travelling companions. Thank you all for the great times we had together, out there in the Outback.

And to my husband Renato, who goes the extra mile with me, and takes the photographs to prove it.

CONTENTS

PART I: The Anne Beadell Highway

Hitting the Road. 1
The Painted Desert 9
White Man's Holes 13
Dog Fence Camp 14
Death Adder Camp 19
Maggie's Run Camp 20
Spinifex Camp. 22
Damp Camp. 24
Mother's Day Camp 24
Connie Sue Camp 25
Quarantine Camp 27

PART II: The Canning Stock Route

Friday 13th Camp: Well 6 31
Midnight Special Camp: Well 12. 37
Murray Rankin's Trolley Camp: Well 15 40
Durba Springs: Near Well 17. 42
Lake Disappointment Heights Camp: Near Well 20 46
Pit Bull Camp: Well 24 47
Full Moon Camp: Well 21 51
Fly Camp: Well 31 52
Halfway Camp: Well 35 53
Desert Oak Camp: Just past Well 39 57
Boiling Billy Camp: Well 42 61
Moet Camp: Well 46 63
Six Can Camp: Well 49 66
Termite Dating Camp: Stretch Lake 69

PART III: The Mighty Mitchell Plateau

    5,000 Burgers 71
    Gwion Gwion. 74
    Honeymoon Bay 76

PART IV: The Hay River Track

    Back to Birdsville. 81
    North of Big Red 83
    Boulia or Bust 88
    Dinosaur Country 90
    Banjo Mania 91
    Revenge 92
    Cobbold Gorge. 93

PART V: Cape York

    Roadside Repairs. 95
    The Crazy CREB Track 98
    The Darwin Award. 99
    Gollums. 101
    The OTT 104
    The Tip 107
    Not the Frenchman's Track 110
    Lockhart Art 114
    Chilli Beach. 117
    Drongos. 119
    Emerald Water 122

PART VI: Arnhem Land and The Top End

    Jurassic Park 127
    What a Croc! 132

Glossary of Terms: Australian English 137
About Sam Mitchell. 141
About the Author 141
More Books by Maggie Ramsay 143

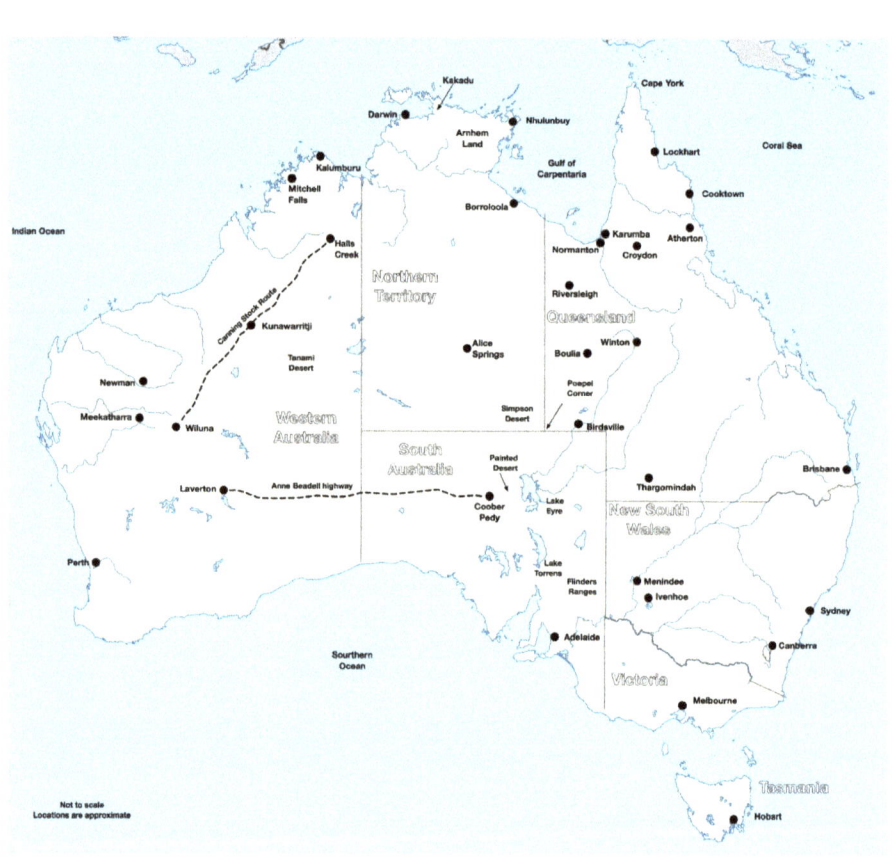

PART I

THE ANNE BEADELL HIGHWAY

Hitting the Road

Take a couple of discarded wooden pallets, dry as corn husks, and turn them into a raging fire. Put a big yellow moon behind, rising above a smooth little dam and laying a path of golden light across the water. Then just above it all, put the Southern Cross. Yep, day 1 on the road, headin' directly west from Sydney into the vast, remote Australian Outback and it's taking shape nicely.

Of course, as we are on our way to tackle five of the continent's toughest tracks and some of the harshest territory imaginable, it will undoubtedly throw up plenty of challenges and some hair-raising surprises. But we are easing into it.

Tiny Temora, 420 kilometres west of Sydney, has one attraction—two World War II Spitfires and an annual airshow. Maybe they are practising or just having a bit of a joyride, but when we stop for lunch beside the new tourist lake there is one up there doing death-defying stunts. A little, single-engine, striped plane with a pilot who obviously was born without the capacity for fear. Try climbing vertically to a great height until you stall, then drop directly down, spinning over and over until the engine coughs and you swerve out of it just before you hit the ground. Thanks for the private show, Temora.

100 years ago, Banjo Patterson, Australia's favourite bush poet, wrote down an old song, "Flash Jack from Gundagai." It is mostly a list of all the places where Flash Jack was a gun shearer, the fastest in the shed.

So, the first time we camped at an abandoned homestead near Hay in far south-western New South Wales a few years ago, I had been ridiculously pleased to discover that this very place, Willandra, figures in that list of the famous stations in the era when Australia rode to prosperity on the sheep's back.

After the shearing, after the wool clip had been baled and sold and shipped off to Europe, the station owners would load their family up and go to a capital city to spend up big on cars and holidays, clothes for the missus and some new furniture for the farmhouse. They were the glory days of these homesteads and the image of the nation.

> "I've shore at Burrabogie and I've shore at Toganmain
> I've shore at big Willandra and out on the Coleraine
> But before the shearing was over I wished I was back again
> Shearin' for old Tom Patterson, on the One-Tree Plain
>
> All among the wool, boys, all among the wool
> Keep your blades full, boys, keep your blades full
> I can do a respectable tally meself whenever I like to try
> And I'm known around the country as Flash Jack from Gundagai…"

The sprawling farmhouse at Willandra with its wide verandas and old palm trees looks as if the family has just gone out for the day. There is still the solid old furniture in the rooms, all turned arms and tapestry seats. The pictures still hang on the walls and the framed photographs of gigantic prize-winning rams from its heyday have pride of place over the mantelpiece.

We liked Willandra so much that we usually come here on our way to the west, and spend a night camped here, wandering around, soaking up the pioneering feeling.

Ivanhoe is the next little town, with a chunky, no-nonsense policewoman ("G'day mate"), and Wendy with a lot of blonde hair at the servo

("Mornin' luv"). We've met Wendy before, and she has always been very friendly and chatty, but she is now high on our long list of Outback good-deeds people. 100 kilometres along the road to Menindee, on a previous trip, we got a phone call (a fluke in itself so far from anywhere, just a momentary patch of coverage).

"Were you just in here?" she asked. She had found my wallet, hunted through it, found a possible phone number and gave it a go. It was a 200-kilometre roundtrip to collect it, but what the heck.

This stretch of road has form for us. A couple of years ago we got hopelessly bogged halfway along it. Up to our axles in gluggy clay. Our feet slipping and sliding on mud so slick it was like ice. So bogged that we had to spend the night right there stuck on the road and thought it might be a week. We christened it Mud Camp. We were with friends, and heading for the next big town, Broken Hill, where Nonie was going to do a phone interview for a job she really, really wanted.

Instead, stuck in that mud miles from anywhere she, in desperation, had to do the interview right there on the satellite phone. Ren was standing up on top of the roof rack holding the sat phone high in the air to get a signal, with his arm up, looking like a photo of a mountaineer who had just summited Everest.

Nonie was crouched down below, leaning on the bull bar, in muddy shorts and gumboots, trying to sound confident and professional, while also trying to deal with the unsettling lags in the conversation on a sat phone as the sound flies up to the satellite and down again. But don't ever underestimate Nonie in any tricky situation—she got the job.

The next morning Stuart had spotted a couple of young hillbilly blokes walking in.

"We've got company," he announced. Two young blokes straggled in.

"We're bogged down the road," they explained, "but we need to get to Ivanhoe—for bail report at the police station."

Suddenly we were on high alert. What were they charged with? Were we marooned out here, miles from any help, with serious criminals? We chatted on carefully, all ears for any hints. But it was nothing very serious, it turned out when we heard the story. They were just a couple of kids who had been letting off steam a bit too wildly and went too far.

They told us their Pop was nearby on his farm. "Give him a ring," they said confidently. "He'll come and drag us out." We all settled down to spin a few yarns for a while and eventually Pop arrived in a beat-up old ute. He had shoulder-length white hair and a huge beard and was covered with tattoos. He looked the scene over, spat contemptuously into a nearby bush, gave the boys a scathing look and backed into position.

With a lot of gunning of his motor and spinning tyres, and probably terminal damage to his clutch, he managed to drag us out. Then little Outback Ivanhoe came up trumps again, when the Fire Station let us use their high-pressure hose to get all the glutinous mud off our rigs. It took half an hour of scrubbing before we were finished.

The road leads on to Menindee Lakes in far western New South Wales, which used to be a lovely camping spot beside the water. People came from Broken Hill in droves for fishing and boating. There were flocks of pelicans sailing serenely past. Now, to our astonishment, the lakes have been drained, to send the water downstream. The lake-bed is now scrubby undergrowth with actual camels walking around on it. What? Why? We sit staring forlornly at what used to be our nice waterfront campsite as the sun goes down.

We are heading for the Flinders Ranges. This is one of the treasures of the Outback. A saw-toothed range lines the horizon and the steep hills are striped with bony ridges of rock that look like the backs of dinosaurs.

The Flinders has a spectacular set of gorges. They show the power of eons, with lines of multi-coloured ochre rock heaved up to lie in great slanted cliffs. They are some of the oldest geological formations on the planet, between 500 and 800 million years old.

Wilpena Pound is the most visited place here, a massive curved bowl of hills. The early settlers were able to safely keep their cattle here, so they called it a pound. It is a natural wonder, like an amphitheatre. It is best viewed from above, after a long climb past the old stone farmhouse with its story of back-breaking work and impossible battles with nature, and up a long set of steps.

There is a viewing platform at the top where you can see how the hills scoop down to the centre where once the cattle grazed. At Wilpena the flow of tourists has created a local industry. There is a Visitor Information Centre, gift shop, motel and camping ground, mostly staffed by Indigenous people from the area.

If a picture is worth a thousand words, Hans Heyson should do it for you. Fresh from the green fields of Europe he stumbled on the gritty scenery of the Flinders in 1926, set up his easel and never really left. His paintings lovingly capture the landscape's unique beauty. And like him, we just keep coming back for another look.

We do, however, seem to have worked our special magic on the weather. We are famous for our talent in breaking droughts when we travel and lying in bed last night we heard the first little pitter-pat on the canvas. Not wanting to be stranded in another Mud Camp we scrambled to pack everything we could in case of a hasty getaway, then tossed restlessly through the night as little showers came and went. Just before dawn, with the rain getting steadier, we threw our last few things together and left in the dark.

It is emu country now and if an emu had a name it would be Beryl. Or maybe Doris. They could so easily be trotting into an RSL club ready to have a little shandy and a game of bingo and a bit of a gossip. In real life they flounce away picking up their long legs and bouncing their feathery backsides.

People wonder what there is to see in the vast Australian Outback but apart from the emus and kangaroos there is a surprising amount to look at along this desolate road to Coober Pedy.

There is Lake Eyre of course, which is twelve metres below sea level, and is usually just a crust of dried salt to the horizon. It has had actual rain recently which has led to it having actual water in it. This is very unusual. Once-in-a hundred-years kind of unusual. The sightseeing pilots must be raking it in, because apart from knowing the water might be out there, all you see from the edge is still the same as before: a silver swathe of salt crystals.

Along the road a bit further there are ochre pits, deep hollows of striking red, orange, yellow and white clay which has been dug up and traded by the local Indigenous people from around 60,000 years ago until right now. You can stand at the edge and imagine all those centuries of people down there digging it up, putting it in their dilly bags and heading for the next nice big slab of rock face to start painting.

The next attraction is the ruins of Farina. It was founded in 1878 and destined to be a major town, or so the early settlers believed. Farina was busy for a while as the railhead—Sidney Kidman, the Cattle King, put 30,000 cattle onto the trains there in 1909 alone, bringing them through every week in mobs of about 300 to drip feed the market in Adelaide.

But the promise of cropping wheat there (hence the name Farina) couldn't succeed against the lack of reliable rainfall, or mostly any rainfall at all. Eventually there was just one family there, with all the old buildings derelict. Then in 2009 a few hardy enthusiasts decided to restore what was left of the town.

They firstly, in an inspired moment, decided to get the old underground bakery into working order. Now, using volunteer labour and led by an ex-navy baker, they are providing most of the funds for the restorations by selling bread, finger buns, sausage rolls and meat pies to tourists as fast as they can come out of the old oven. We look around, wrap ourselves around some of the finger buns and then head off down the road.

What would you do if you had a couple of old planes? Stand them on their tails, of course, and while you are at it, build a few huge weird statues out of scrap metal: a man with a child in his arm, a huge flower, a dog made out of a massive water tank. Some bizarre person did this, way out here, and it is irresistible to stop and gawk at them. The Outback attracts eccentrics, that's one of its charms.

That nutty sculpture garden in the middle of nowhere is no crazier, I guess, than having a black-tie ball at the abandoned railway siding at Curdimurka. We stop for a look. It is just a tiny brick building standing alone in the enormous empty landscape, beside some rusty railway tracks. But every two years it springs to life. People come from all over the world to dance the night away on tarpaulins spread out underfoot on the red dirt, with the great bowl of stars above.

Just up the road, in the middle of this dry desert landscape, is another surprise. Water from far underground makes its way to the surface, taking a couple of million years to get there. The ground is dotted with hillocks: mound springs. Each one has a bubbling hot pool at the top, steaming and popping as the water breaks through from far, far away underground. Every bubble is uncountably old. There are animals and plants that only occur on each single mound, and nowhere else on earth. What a country! You would think there is nothing much here in this vast empty-looking space, but we are constantly gasping with surprise.

We are a long way from anywhere when we come across Neil. He is wiry and grimy, with torn shorts and an ancient Akubra hat. He is lounging in a camp chair beside the road, having a smoke. He could be anything from 50 to 70, impossible to tell. His battered old ute, loaded with gear, is parked on the edge of the road.

"You all right?" we ask.

"Yeah, just a bit of a problem with me car."

Turns out he has a collapsed wheel bearing and a broken axle.

"Me mate in New South Wales is chasin' up some parts from a wreckers' and sendin' them up to me," he says cheerfully.

"Do you need anything, you ok for food?"

"Yeah, I'm only short of smokes and beer. I'd get the publican up at William Creek to send some to me, but I've only got $50."

We couldn't help with the smokes, but we left him with some beers. He'll probably be there for a month, sitting beside the road, and there's a good chance that old ute will never move from that spot.

When we get to William Creek, 30 kilometres up the road, we check at the pub. Yes, they know he is down the road and they won't let him die out there. This is a typical Outback pub with a lot of character: there is even a signed photo from actor Paul Hogan, star of the iconic movie Crocodile Dundee, hanging on the wall.

And the pub itself had a role in the movie Last Cab to Darwin. With its typical Outback décor, they didn't need to build a set to create the slightly-crackers atmosphere. Last time we were here a tree outside was hung with what looked like a dozen mummified cats. After a horrified first glance we had realised that they were actually movie props made of papier mache. Nice touch. This time in William Creek they are all gone, souvenired of course.

This is a massive country. Anna Creek is nearby, the largest cattle station in the world. It has an area of more than 34,000 square kilometres. It is so big that it is actually larger than Israel, larger than Belgium. And it is not only massive, but it is hostile.

Here is where the warning signs start: "You are entering a remote area," they declare sternly. "If you break down do not leave your car." There is a list of other handy hints to try to avoid leaving your bleached bones out there. As you stand reading the notice and gaze ahead to the horizon with absolutely nothing in between, it does tend to put a thoughtful look on your face. A sort of, "Do we have enough water?" look.

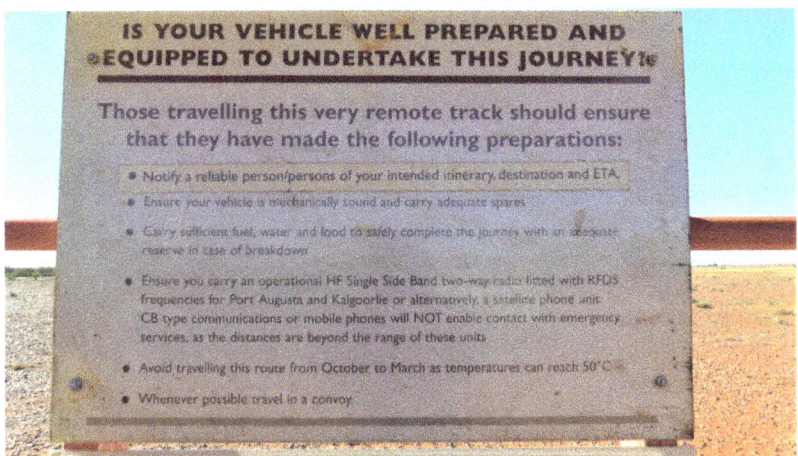

THE PAINTED DESERT

Thousands of kilometres from any of the cities perched on the coast, and distant even from the dry, dusty towns of the inland, right in the heart of the continent, lies an astonishing and magical place, The Painted Desert.

It is 250 kilometres north of Anna Creek Station, and it is very small and very far away from anywhere else, but it has a mystique all its own. The gateway is Oodnadatta, a scrabble of corrugated iron buildings dominated by the Pink Roadhouse. That building is quite a sight: bright pink, Barbie pink, with a pink car permanently parked at the fuel pumps.

The same Aboriginal man always sits strumming a guitar and singing a Country and Western song in the shade of the wide veranda. A scrum of chocolate-coloured kids kick a ball around in the dust. Behind the counter are the two predictable sights of the Outback pub: a down-to-earth girl wearing riding boots and a t-shirt branded by a beer company, and a blonde twenty-something Scandinavian on a working holiday.

A hundred kilometres South-West of Oodna, as the locals call it, is our quarry. It is late afternoon by the time we reach the area, and it has been blowing a fierce, exhausting gale all day, ramping up the fuel

consumption and making every step outside the car a misery. So we see a flash of hills and rocks go by, but push on past it to Arckaringa Homestead. This is the only place where it is permitted to camp on the vast property, and we plan to spend a few days exploring.

As we pull up to the house, a little boy runs out.

"Have you got any kids?" he calls hopefully. "I haven't had anyone to play with for ages."

We can't help with playmates, but we do buy a piece of shiny silver gypsum from him for $2. He's a good little businessman—at this rate he could possibly afford to fly some friends in pretty soon.

His mother appears, wearily pushing a lock of hair back from her forehead and squinting in the bright sunlight.

"Where is the Painted Desert?" we ask.

"You've just driven through it," she says. She is polite and friendly, but it is obviously something she has repeated a thousand times.

Is that it? Did we come all this way just for that? We had expected to spend days driving around in it. We unpack the camper trailer, lash everything down against the fierce wind, and hunker down, a bit disappointed. Since we're already here, though, and we have come so far to see it, the next morning we decide to backtrack and have another look, just in case there is something worth seeing.

We drive back the ten kilometres. To our surprise, in the morning light and with no gale blowing, we are really struck by it. It has a startling beauty. And that first impression just gets better and better. This is a tiny, pocket-sized gem.

Nature has endowed a set of rocky hills with an exquisite array of colours. Black, rusty brown, red, pink, gold and grey, as if a giant paintbox has upended and the colours have flowed down in streaks and splashes. It is not the strident, exuberant orange of so many parts of the inland—this is more subtle, more varied.

The ground is covered in stones, one patch of colour here, changing abruptly to another there. Every sloping hillside of stony scree is washed in the colour palette of the Outback. And actually, part of the charm is that the scale is so small; it is just a few patches of hills.

The only walk listed on a home-made sign is just two kilometres long. It takes us to the top of one crest, and along a bony little ridge, where it stops abruptly. But it is enough. We can look down at the brilliant hues, a different colour in every direction, all around us. It is absolutely enchanting.

The next day we toss up heading straight for Coober Pedy. After all, the farmer's wife has said there is nothing more to see. But, out of curiosity we decide that we might as well do the loop we first intended, from Arckaringa west to Copper Hills station and then south to Evelyn Downs.

Anna Creek, Evelyn Downs—these gentle place names are deceptive. The properties are truly gigantic. All over the Outback you can pass a sign giving the name of a farm that sounds like something in rural England, and then drive for 50 or 100 kilometres before you reach the other boundary.

But we are used to these big places. What we are not expecting is that the beautiful cluster of hills that had surprised us in the Painted Desert continues, line after line, those lovely dusky pinks and golds with the flat mesa tops and rocky outcrops, in every direction.

Even the ground between the hills is multi-coloured. What was the farmer's wife thinking? Maybe she has never been in this direction, always heading for Oodna in her rare trips off the property and doesn't know that it goes on and on like this. Surely not. We spend all morning in a series of exclamations, punctuated with stops to take photographs.

Then, abruptly, the landscape changes. What was the Painted Desert turns into what should be called the Moon Desert. Imagine the barren surface of the moon but completely flat, dead brown, and covered with stones the size of a blueberry muffin. Not a tree, not a tuft of green, not a single hill. Dead flat.

That's the surreal landscape we are suddenly looking at. Nothing but a carpet of brown stones to the horizon, broken here and there by a flash of the silvery shine of flakes of gypsum. No muffins, though, nothing edible as far as the eye can see.

No wonder so many movies have been filmed between Oodnadatta and Coober Pedy—Mad Max and Priscilla Queen of the Desert to name just a couple—that have displayed these bizarre, compelling landscapes to the world.

There is no wildlife to be seen at all, not even birds. Almost everywhere, no matter how barren the landscape, there is usually a hawk circling lazily above on the lookout for some tiny mouse, but here there is nothing; the sky is bare, a hard, shiny blue.

But somewhere, lurking out there, are the fearsome Perentie Lizards. They are just like a normal cute little lizard whisking charmingly around your garden, but here two metres long and half a metre round the middle. Try looking up from your sandwich to find yourself eye to eye with one of those.

And that's not only the scary thing around here. I slide on some loose stones at the side of the road, put my hand down and get a sharp little burr in it, like a bindi-eye. It's nothing, I just pull it out.

But it hurts, it really hurts, and within seconds of me pulling it out, my hand starts to swell, all the veins stand out, and I am shaking and shivering and feeling dizzy and nauseous. Ren eyes me anxiously and makes a note to get an Epi-pen for the first aid kit. That little burr must have carried a shot of vicious toxin in its tiny tip. It didn't kill me, and the angry red welt gradually settled down over the next few days, but I was on full alert from then on for innocent-looking little burrs. It's a harsh country.

White Man's Holes

We are heading for Coober Pedy, the opal mining town, which has its own quaint warning signs like "Don't walk backwards." There is a good reason for that—the whole area is pitted with mine shafts. The town is a magnet for loners who live in houses dug underground and who prospect for the local white-toned opal. This prospecting activity gives the town a unique moonscape effect, surrounded by hummocks of slag, and every hill has a door opening into it, where a miner has hollowed out a cool cavern home to escape the ferocious summer heat.

Remember the first Mad Max movie? All those crazies wearing leather armour roaming around a post-apocalyptic wasteland in terrifying vehicles? It was filmed just thirty kilometres out of Coober Pedy at a place called The Breakaways. This spectacular landscape was a perfect setting for that movie, and it is stunning to visit.

From the top of a mesa, the land falls away in great swoops of stark orange and red rock, with a bare flat plain in between. It is the site of the dystopian wars between the survivors of The Great Catastrophe. Surreal? So is Coober Pedy, it's a perfect match.

When the police station in the town was built they had to put wire mesh around the foundations to stop local wits from rolling dynamite underneath the building. That probably gives you a clue.

Coober Pedy is Aboriginal for "White Man's Holes". It is entertaining to visit, to exclaim at its wackiness. But live here? Even stay more than a night? Umm… no! It's time to move on.

Dog Fence Camp

When your destination for the day is the Dog Fence, you know you are definitely heading way out there. We wave goodbye to Coober Pedy with its raffish air, its nutty eccentrics and its grizzled old-timers. On the way out, we go back for another look at the Mad Max Breakaways.

It is irresistible to gaze one more time at that spectacular sight. The sloping ochre cliffs striped with low bushes look as if they are streaming away into the distant plain far below.

Then we turn and point ourselves due west into the Great Victoria Desert. The Vic is one of the most remote and inhospitable places on this largely life-threatening continent. When we wave goodbye to Coober Pedy we also wave goodbye to mail, phone, internet, shops, water supply, diesel and, apart from the Flying Doctor, medical help (and even that could take hours, if not days, to reach us.).

Everyone we had spoken to in Coober Pedy about the track shook their head and said, in that gloomy voice of the habitual pessimist, "Good luck mate, a bloke I know went out there and wrecked his car. Another vehicle behind him broke as well. And the guy with the rescue truck didn't make it either."

They love throwing out these dire warnings, leaning on the counter of their mechanic's workshop or tyre place, and all you can do is stick your fingers in your ears and say, "La-la-la," because if you listened to them you would never move out of your lounge room.

This time, though, it got to me. I lay awake thinking, "This was my idea, and I've talked Ren and our friends into doing this and tomorrow we are going to set out and our cars will break and, and, and—and it will be All My Fault. But, never ventured etc. Next morning the sun is shining, the track beckons and we head off to find out for ourselves.

There is plenty of promise of misery and disaster right from the start. Every kilometre becomes more arid, more stony, with little shiny brown gibbers scattered thickly across the bare ground, and just a few scraggly bushes dotted here and there. It is all a palette of red and brown.

Near Mabel Creek, an Aboriginal Community 50 kilometres along (with no alcohol and no unauthorised access to the community) the track crosses the railway line. The famous tourist train The Ghan goes through here from Adelaide to Darwin, a 3000-kilometre line crossing the content from south to north with just two stops along the way.

It used to be called "The Afghan Express" after the camel drivers who ran teams of camels in the nineteenth century. They carted the supplies to the properties and towns before the roads went through and trucks took over. The "Afghans" were actually mostly Indians, but they were always known as Afghans and, let's face it, "The Ghan" wouldn't sound nearly as exotic if it was "The Ind."

There are still remains of the old camel trains—the Outback is full of wild camels. They are thriving so much that they are now a lucrative trade for many properties, exported to the Middle East as racing camels, highly sought-after breeding stock, and meat. They are also an environmental pest, particularly as they ruin waterholes by padding around, drinking a lot and sometimes falling in and dying there, fouling the water.

But they are very quaint and entertaining to see as they plod solemnly onto the track in front of your vehicle. They are big. And wild. I wonder what sort of person is able to round up wild camels and persuade them to walk onto a truck? They sure breed blokes tough out here.

Talking of tough, John McDouall Stuart was the first European to explore this area. He came through in 1859. How hard must that have been! This is incredibly difficult country to survive in, with temperatures at ground level sometimes reaching 65 degrees Celsius in summer (149 degrees Fahrenheit) and with virtually no water, but he somehow lived to tell the tale. The Stuart Highway between Adelaide and Darwin bears his name.

And here's another extraordinary character: Len Beadell. There was a panicky moment during the Second World War when a Japanese soldier was captured, and it was discovered that he had a map with more detail about Darwin and its surrounds than the Australian government's own maps.

Darwin is Australia's most northerly city and it was in the direct line of the rapidly advancing Japanese army. Suddenly an alarm went off in Canberra, Australia's capital city and seat of the Federal government. Someone woke up to the idea that it might be smart to find out what was actually out in the Outback, in detail. And make some roads out there, just in case.

What they needed was someone who was a brilliant surveyor, a perfectionist, a whizz with a sextant, willing to work in extremely harsh and lonely conditions and with a taste for the desert. They found the perfect person in Len Beadell.

For twenty years from the early 1950s he plotted a network of tracks all through the centre of Australia, using old-fashioned instruments and working with a team of just three assistants—a bulldozer driver, a grader driver and a cook.

His brilliant surveying skills resulted in perfect calculations that have, without exception, been proved accurate using modern GPS technology. His markers are all along his routes: crosses on the ground made of rocks with Department of Lands medallions in the centre; carefully annotated signs on posts with distances, coordinates, and arrows neatly stamped by hand into a sheet of metal.

He deserves to be famous—he is truly one of the great explorers of this continent. No-one in the cities has heard of him and he doesn't appear in any histories of exploration. For the Outback traveller, though, Len is a hero. In two places along the Anne Beadell there is a tin box with a notebook and a couple of ballpoint pens inside. They are there for travellers' messages, as well as names, dates, destinations and comments, and those books have a lot of, "Thanks Len" scrawled in them.

The Gunbarrel Highway is one of his roads, along with a set of tracks named, very touchingly, after members of his family. One of these, the Anne Beadell Highway, honours his wife and is our current thrill.

This lonely track has a fearsome reputation. Despite its name, it ain't no highway as you might imagine a highway. It is 1300 kilometres of ferocious corrugations, startling washouts and soft sandy hollows that runs in an almost straight line from just west of Coober Pedy to the centre of Western Australia, across claypans, sand dunes, salt lakes and rocky outcrops. Most of it has not been graded since it was made in the 1950s and even then it was just a track bulldozed, graded and left to its own devices ever since.

Our previous trip to this part of the world was back in 2011. That time, looking longingly at the map, we had had to turn back at the very start, beaten by storms far to the north that were sending floodwaters steadily towards us from a cyclone and fierce thunderstorms. Not the track to traverse alone, or in flood conditions, so we abandoned the attempt. For then…

Now the weather forecast looks safe and we are travelling with friends, the intrepid Nonie and Stuart, who have developed the same strange fascination with the wild beauty and isolation of the Outback that keeps us coming back.

Death Adder Camp

Here's a handy hint for fitness in the Outback: run past a snake. It is guaranteed to lift your heart rate and make you run a whole lot faster. Ren puts it to the test when he is out jogging today.

Death Adders are a short, fat, evil-looking snake with a flat shovel-shaped head. They dig themselves into the warm soft earth, or hide under a pile of leaves, in a traffic path for small animals. They lie in wait, motionless, just leaving the skinny end of their tail sticking out, wiggling to attract prey. As the unsuspecting marsupial mouse or little bird comes in close for a look, the vibrations of its feet in the dirt tell the snake that it's dinner time and—zap, the adder strikes!

Ren catches a glimpse of one while he is out jogging. He spots its beady little eyes fixed on him as he runs past. He survives that encounter. But then he realises that has to run past it back to camp. He lives to tell the tale, but the bottle of Scotch gets a fair bit of damage.

It does of course result in a fear in all of us of going outside to commune with nature during the night, when it is dark and snakes are out hunting.

Want to know how remote it is here? This should give you a clue: it is the most remote location the British could find when they were looking for an extremely isolated place to test their atomic bombs in the 1950s, when the Cold War began. Remember that at that time the British still controlled big chunks of the planet, so they had plenty of places to choose from. But this was the spot they finally settled on.

The site is still a prohibited area being, of course, still radioactive and it is necessary to get a permit even to visit. It is an eerie place. Close to ground zero there is a ring of signs about fifty metres apart telling the local Indigenous people not to camp or hunt for food there (although, to our national shame, at the time of the explosions there were Indigenous people simply left in the area).

You can drive right to the spot where it all happened (making jokes, of course, about glowing in the dark and did you bring the Geiger counter). All that is left at the centre now is some twisted metal, six blocks of concrete that held down some Mustang planes that were part of the tests, a couple of obelisks giving the dates of the explosions, and the remains of the camera supports.

A few kilometres away is an observation point on a low hill. I guess in those more innocent days walking back a bit and holding your hat up was considered enough protection against the radiation from the blast.

It is a spooky feeling to imagine that mushroom cloud billowing up right there. Not a place to linger too long. We take our photos and get out of there.

Maggie's Run Camp

When we pull off the road this afternoon to make camp I decide to go for a run. People who watch horror movies to frighten themselves should, if they really want to scare themselves silly, take a jog along a sandy track as night falls, wondering at every step if a death adder is going to rear up out of the gloom and bite them on the ankle.

Note to self: don't run so close to dusk next time. In fact, probably the best decision would be to sit down with a good book and a bar of chocolate instead of running at all.

But I do run—if trotting along, staring at the ground and shying away from every stick counts as running. There are dark little hollows, and piles of just the sort of leaves that death adders love to hide in. The setting sun casts long thin shadows exactly like brown snakes; and brown snakes are the sort of vicious creatures that don't lie in wait, but instead chase and strike. And there might be some of the dreaded taipans, almost the deadliest snakes on earth, lying in wait. I trip and gasp and jump, and finally turn tail and race back to camp, with a pounding heart and ragged breath.

After surviving that frightening run, what helps bring the heart rate down and makes everything seem ok again is to relax by a big cheery campfire, have a glass of red and eat a fabulous meal of butterflied roast lamb cooked on the fire with potatoes, carrots, onions and parsnips baked in the embers.

This is an amazing track. It is just as wild, rough and tough as everyone says, but it is also absolutely gorgeous. The vegetation changes every few kilometres, with bushes, trees and low grasses stretching away to the horizon. The trees are grey-green and the sandy soil is burnt orange.

There has been some very rare rain recently and during the day we meet some people coming from the west who tell us that the road has been closed at Laverton, near the other end. They had been held up for a couple of days while the rain passed over and the track dried out. So this is probably greener than usual and there are wildflowers everywhere—the tiny, hardy little flowers of the desert that spring up when there is a drop of rain and vanish just as fast.

This is also spinifex country; the locals call themselves the Spinifex People. Those delicate grasses that look so pretty from the car, waving and glistening in the sunlight, are vicious little devils when you meet them up close. Each tussock is tipped with hundreds of filaments, needle-sharp spikes that effortlessly poke through trousers and into skin. Put your hand on one accidentally and you will have dozens of sore spots that last for days. (How do I know this? Yep). And make your campfire too close to one and the flammable oils in them can blaze through to the horizon in a flash—literally.

Spinifex Camp / Unnamed Conservation Park Camp / Just Outside the Culturally Sensitive Area Camp

How do the French do it? We met a delightful, adventurous and intrepid young French couple, Michel and Marie, a few days ago and then again today. They are travelling rough in an ancient Land Rover in the same dusty brown landscape as us. They even drove their vehicle from Australia to Europe a few years ago. So they have a thirst for adventure and they don't mind roughing it.

But somehow they always look as if they have just stepped out of the shower and into a set of fresh clothes. Just like people in France always look elegant and chic. When we meet them again on the track and stop for a chat, Marie hops out of the car in her crisp shorts and neat t-shirt, her hair in a jaunty ponytail. Must be something in the air in France that does it, during childhood. Amazing.

Garry, on the other hand, is exactly the opposite. A young bloke who has been working at Port Hedland, on the far north-west coast of Western Australia, he is heading home to Queensland via the Anne Beadell, the Simpson Desert, and the Birdsville Track. As you do. Why go on the bitumen when you can have a bit of excitement instead?

In fact, don't muck around, mate, do three of the toughest tracks you can in one trip. His hair sticks up in tufts and hasn't seen shampoo for weeks, and maybe he hasn't had a shower for that long, either. He has vivid tattoos covering both arms down to the wrists. He is having the time of his life and will have some serious stories to tell his mates.

Then there are the three girls from Sweden who are absolutely caricatures of themselves. You could write a chick-flick starring them, straight out of central casting. There is the chunky, forthright one with a loud voice and no-nonsense shorts; the thin, quiet one with glasses and straight brown hair; and the blonde with long legs, bright pink shorts and, most hilarious of all, a pink fly veil. I tried to think up a title to their movie, but I discovered that anything with "Swedish" in the name sounds vaguely pornographic.

You meet all sorts out here.

As you can see, we are camped at…Undecided Camp, due to unresolved discussion by the various members of the party as to what the name of tonight's campsite should be:

a) Spinifex Camp? There is certainly lots of spinifex—thousands of hectares of it, in strange circular patterns that look like a gigantic maze.

b) Unnamed Conservation Park Camp? The conservation park actually has an official sign at the entrance declaring that it is indeed "Unnamed Conservation Park". Perhaps the locals couldn't agree on a name and eventually some bureaucrat in frustration just said, "Well stuff it then, it can stay Unnamed."

c) Just Outside the Culturally Sensitive Area Camp? We don't know why this section of the road is culturally sensitive, but it is fifty kilometres of track where camping is not allowed, and it is a stretch of the most beautiful, pristine Outback scenery you could imagine, with everything looking sparse and prickly and desert-y of course, but healthy, varied and perfectly landscaped. In a huge area of great natural beauty, this is outstanding.

So we agree that there is something about it that is special. I imagine there are powerful legends attached to this lovely stretch of land that make it culturally sensitive. We camp just outside to respect the wishes of the locals. After all, it is their back yard.

DAMP CAMP

Everyone knows all about the weather out here and is only too willing to share, in fact it is usually the main topic of conversation. We had been told back at the Police Station in Coober Pedy that some rain was coming in from the west and would pass through on Saturday. We can generally make it rain wherever we go camping, but this was going to happen without our help.

So when it starts to sprinkle we are not surprised, it is right on cue. We have just set up camp in time when the heavens open. It buckets down, with wild winds, and water everywhere in big flat puddles.

We all splash around, battening down the hatches, and paddling back and forth between the trailers, getting drenched and laughing stupidly, retreating to Nonie and Stuart's to eat pasta and play Scrabble as the wind lashes the canvas and the rain beats down.

We eventually go to sleep with the storm still raging, but because the ground is sand, and very parched, by morning there is not a trace of last night's weather. The puddles of water have vanished into the dust, the ground is dry and the sky is again a brilliant enamel blue.

MOTHER'S DAY CAMP

Ilkurlka (try saying that ten times very fast) is a lonely roadhouse that has been built about halfway along the Anne Beadell, mainly to service the needs of the Tjantjantara Aboriginal community who live just down their private road a bit to the south (130 kilometres just down the road, that is).

It is, as well, a handy place for the occasional vehicle to stop. There is diesel for sale, for one thing. Before that travellers had to organise a fuel drop of a 44-gallon drum, brought in from hundreds of kilometres away at enormous cost. And there is also Phil—quiet, friendly and chatty—who runs the store and is a mine of local information.

He is so isolated that he has to call in to his distant headquarters every morning at a set time, just to let someone know that he is still alive. We keep him busy chatting and posing for photos with him, and while that is happening he misses making one of those calls. Within a few minutes they ring to check.

There is a little shelter shed, a rainwater tank and a metal picnic table at Ilkurlka. There is also, oh bliss, a bore water shower with a donkey engine. These are amazing contraptions—so simple, so practical and, for a worn and dusty traveller, absolute heaven. You heat it up by lighting a little fire of scraps of wood under a tank of water. The fire crackles away, the water heats up and you then luxuriate in a hot alfresco shower. A shower longer than our regular 30 seconds, even long enough to wash your hair. Out there, in that setting, it feels like the height of luxury.

There is also, in the store, alongside the jam and fly spray and UHT milk, a table loaded with paintings by local Indigenous artists. We look, then look some more, then fall for the temptation and buy one, along with a certificate of authenticity and a short bio of the artist.

Ren had planned to buy some art this trip, and I do really like what we have chosen, but a little voice in my head is saying, "I hope it's not like when you go to Bali." You know how it is, you buy a batik shirt that looks so great there but when you get it home it's, "Oh no, what was I thinking!" We'll see, it will either be in pride of place in our front foyer or tucked away in that dim, dark part of the hall.

Ilkurlka is a welcome rest stop after an exhausting day of bone-jarring corrugations and a bitter westerly wind. We stop early and, as it is Mother's Day, Stuart whips up a treat of high tea with chocolate chip pancakes, UHT cream, and maple syrup. Life's hard.

Connie Sue Camp

Crashing a plane way out here would be a big, big problem. Firstly, how to survive it, followed by how to be rescued. In 1993 a small plane came down with three people on board. Amazingly, they all lived to tell the tale and managed to be rescued; it is almost impossible to calculate the odds of that.

Because of the remoteness of the crash site the insurance company decided that they would just salvage the most valuable parts, like the engine, and leave the rest of the plane there. So even now you can walk right up to it, and peer inside. It is like a ghost ship. It is sitting at a rakish angle on the ground, still with the seats intact and the remnants of the carpet and curtains fluttering in the breeze. It would be really creepy except for the unlikely fact that nobody died.

There are a few other wrecks along the track—a couple of car bodies are rusting away in the scrub and there are two sad camper trailers, certainly not built for this extreme punishment, that have been abandoned. They would have been fun at a caravan park near the beach, but they definitely spoiled their owner's holiday out here.

The first road Len Beadell created out of the virgin scrub was the Gunbarrel Highway to the north of here. His team called it that because they basically just pointed in a straight line west and went for it. Another one of Len's roads runs north to south between the Gunbarrel and the Anne Beadell. Len and Anne travelled that track as he was building the road, with their baby daughter who was just two months old when they started. Naturally Len named it after that little girl: The Connie Sue Highway.

Anne died in 2010, and Connie Sue has put up a memorial plaque to her mother along the Anne Beadell. She also regularly puts new visitor books in the two tin boxes along the track, with notes of welcome to travellers, and an "RIP Mum" in one of them. It is very personal and sweet; that family really owns these tracks.

We camp at the crossroads of the Anne Beadell and the Connie Sue, at Neale Junction, so of course it has to be called the Connie Sue Camp.

Quarantine Camp

This is the last night on the Anne Beadell, always a bittersweet moment out here. Relief at having made it intact but regret that the adventure is over. Tomorrow we will finish in Laverton, deep in the heart of Western Australia. The road has improved steadily ever since Ilkurlka and is now flat, smooth gravel, graded occasionally. It feels amazing to not be climbing in and out of ruts. There are some road signs starting to appear, mostly picturing a cow, not something you want to hit at full speed. And there are unfriendly Keep Out notices from a mining company.

It is still too marginal for anything pastoral to succeed—the last property here, Yeo, was abandoned years ago. The two-room homestead is still standing with the bucket and pulley shower outside. The old chook pens have some remnants of chicken wire hanging crazily from the uprights. There is a well with a hand-pump and a ladder in the well for the snakes that fall in to climb up. We do a double-take.

"Don't climb down the ladder," a sign warns, or you might meet a venomous snake coming up. Noted.

We love that quaint sign, and this one too, beside the road yesterday: "Quarantine. Do not bring any fruit or vegetables into Western Australia. If you have any, eat them now!"

We have a last look at the vast plain and lovely landscape from the vantage point of Bishop Riley's Pulpit. In a thousand kilometres of almost totally flat land, this rocky plug standing 393 metres above the ground sticks out like…never mind. Of course, Nonie and Stuart take off at a trot to the top. We follow them, climb to the summit and gaze around, taking it in, like who was it gazing out silent upon a peak in Darien? Oh yeah, that's right, it was Cortez, "When with eagle eyes, he star'd at the Pacific—and all his men, look'd at each other with a wild surmise."

Every day of this route has been a feast of sensations. The truly awful road surface threatening to shake our vehicles to pieces has made us drive, very often, at not much more than walking speed, easing over the teeth-rattling corrugations and climbing carefully in and out of the ruts and washouts. It has taken nine days to cover 1300 kilometres.

That has given us plenty of time to appreciate the vivid red and brown ochre colours, the earth and bush scents and the stunning rock and sand scenery. At night the sky has been full of stars, silver against the inky black. It is fascinating and beautiful, and we have loved every moment of it.

Now, on to the Canning Stock Route, following the nomad trail north to the heat, and flies, and ants and…

PART II

THE CANNING STOCK ROUTE

FRIDAY 13TH CAMP: WELL 6

Is it a good idea to start out on Friday the 13th? Tempting fate, we take no notice, throw caution to the wind and hit the road.

The Canning starts in Wiluna. You think you've never heard of Wiluna, but if you have seen the movie "The Rabbit-Proof Fence," that is one of the places that figure in that tragic and stirring story of courage and daring. Australia's generally cheery story of convicts-made-good, our larrikin image and the peaceful multiculturalism of recent times conveniently hides a great national stain.

For around 60 years, from 1910, part-Aboriginal children were taken from their mothers and put into orphanages. Obviously that went horribly wrong, and it is now known as the Stolen Generations. It is recognised as a tragedy for those individuals and beyond that their whole community, but it is also a cause for shame and heartfelt apology from the rest of the population.

The Rabbit-Proof Fence is the true story of a brave and daring young Aboriginal girl who ran away from the orphanage with her sisters and walked 2,400 kilometres to get home to Jigalong, far away to the north and deep in the desert, following the fence as a guide.

Wiluna is one of the spots along the way, just a speck in the boundless landscape, sort of near Meekatharra, sort of near Newman, not really near anywhere except the start of the Gunbarrel Highway and the Canning.

Wiluna used to have about 9,000 inhabitants during a past mining era, but now it is a tiny town, with a mainly Indigenous community. There is basic housing, a health centre and a school. And, of course, a pub, with a group of Aboriginal people sitting on the ground waiting for opening time.

There is a general store, too. Last time we were here it was pretty dingy; now it has new owners, a Chinese family. Outside the shop the Aboriginal people are yelling to each other, their barefoot kids are running around and the dogs are fighting.

But inside the shelves are spic and span and the staff are a set of smiling, twenty-something Chinese, probably all members of the same family. You have to wonder what they think of living out here with no social life at all. They probably didn't imagine life in Australia quite like this.

Nonie and Stuart do a lap of the town to see the sights. We had been here before and stay put. Thirty seconds later they are back, ready to wave good-bye without a backward glance.

We stayed last night at the Gunbarrel Laager, just out of town. It is a typical working farm: a group of corrugated iron sheds spread haphazardly around a homestead, with a lot of big machinery. There always seems to be the sound of a grader in the background.

"Are you still taking campers?" we had asked, over the phone.

"Yes," Mel replied laconically, "I haven't won the lottery yet." When we meet him, he turns out to be a humourist.

"Is Gill still around?" we ask.

"Yes, the amount she's been eatin', she's almost spherical." Mel, I might add, really is in no position to be throwing stones about that, even as a joke.

"We've been here before," we tell him, "about five years ago."

"I never remember names," he replies with a deceptively straight face, "but I can always forget a face."

There is a set of mining-camp huts called dongas set around a central green patch of lawn. It is typical Outback accommodation—shipping containers with windows and doors cut into the side. In the middle of the lawn are five blokes around a big firepit, having a beer and a yarn. It turns out they have four dirt bikes and a tough-looking ute loaded with spares and fuel. They have done the Canning—or parts of it—six or seven times. Mostly they seem to hammer it, break things, and then abandon the attempt when they are running out of spares (like axles). Then, next year, they come back and have another crack at it.

They will probably roar past, noisy and annoying, along the track as we pick our way gingerly over the ruts and corrugations. What was that story about the tortoise and the hare again? Note to self: don't get too cocky, you've got a long way to go.

Because we are travelling with camper trailers we have to take a detour around the start. The station owner won't let us do the first little bit through his property. So we have a stretch of smooth gravel to begin, before we go in at Well 5. The entrance is via Glen-Ayle, a poverty-stricken-looking farmhouse where we hand over $45 per vehicle for passing through.

John Forrest came through here, exploring, in about 1874. The local people were very hostile by then, realising that these strange-coloured men riding on enormous animals were going to do them no good.

Just a few kilometres from the parched homestead at Glen-Ayle are the remains of a rudimentary fort, a stone hut where Forrest and his men sheltered against the marauding parties of Aboriginal people.

Then in 1908 the Canning Stock route was created to make a droving track to bring cattle from the Kimberley to the markets in the south. The farmers hoped that the long trek would kill the cattle tick that was ruining the industry. It was before tick-resistant exotic breeds of cattle, like the Brahman, were introduced to the tropics.

The stock route stretches for 2000 kilometres from Wiluna in the south to Halls Creek at its northern end. Of course, being Australia, they were also on the lookout for mineral deposits. We have always loved to dig stuff up, from the days of the goldrushes onwards.

Along its huge length it traverses six different bio-regions, all variations of the arid environment. Ten different species of spinifex grow here. There are many types of woodland vegetation such as mulga, desert oak and eucalyptus, together with animal life, mostly small and nocturnal: wallabies, echidnas, bilbies, lots of snakes and lizards large and small, and many birds.

The stock route follows the traditional water sources—springs and rockholes—of the Western Desert peoples. It is clear that this area has been occupied for at least 60,000 years, and there is a wealth of evidence such as stone artefacts and rock art all the way along, if you know where to look.

The Canning Stock Route has a gruesome history. The first explorers, David Carnegie, seventh son of an English lord, and Lawrence Wells, set out in 1896 in different parties to find a route north.

Two of Wells' men died of dehydration. David Carnegie decided to take a harsher tack. He grabbed some Aboriginal men, put them in chains with neck collars and fed them salt beef until desperate from thirst they finally, reluctantly, revealed the location of the native wells along the way.

Still, Carnegie had a terrible time. Some of his camels died after eating poisonous grass. One of his men accidentally shot himself. He eventually had a major hissy fit and declared the whole central desert region to be completely unsuited to anything whatsoever.

Then Alfred Canning was sent out, with a massive 100 tons of equipment and a team of men, to build a route along the string of water holes, using the same brutal methods as Carnegie to force the Aboriginal people to disclose their water sources.

He set out in March 1908 and a bit over a year later he had created 31 wells, each one a day's droving distance apart from the next and, a man of few words, sent a telegram simply saying, "Work completed—Canning."

Another 23 or so wells were added later but, after all that effort, only a handful of mobs of cattle were ever brought down the track. It was so very remote and because, understandably, the local First Nations people fought back, it was considered too dangerous. It fell into disrepair until the Second World War, when the government decided it would be good to have it useable in case it was needed suddenly to move troops.

But it really only exists now for travellers like us, who like to get far, far away, have a bit of an adventure and see the desolate centre of the continent in all its rugged grandeur. Nothing is ever done to improve it; it never sees a grader and when you decide to traverse it you simply take your chances and hope for the best.

It will take us around three weeks to reach Halls Creek. Between now and then, other than one Aboriginal community half way along, there is nothing at all other than scenery. No facilities, no farms, no telecoms, absolutely nothing for about a thousand kilometres in any direction.

If that sounds harsh, picture this, our first night's camp. There is a grove of ghost gums, the trunks stately and white, gleaming in the moonlight, the foliage feathery and green. There is a well, with a pulley and bucket to fetch water from the dark depths. There is space and silence and peace. It is Pierre Springs, Well 6, and it is so very lovely that we have decided to stay two nights.

There is information about some locals here, on nicely designed rusty metal stands. Like Tommy Ningebong. Born around 1904 he was a renowned stockman. He was a dogger, selling old horses onto the knackery. He was also a sought-after police tracker, able to follow tiny marks in the earth and undergrowth to hunt down criminals. He was widely respected in both the Aboriginal and pastoral communities.

Having worked for many years on stations Tommy eventually saved enough money for his own property—the first Indigenous person to own a pastoral lease in Western Australia. Still called Blue Hill, it is just down the road from here, 134,530 acres in size and a record of one man's courage and determination against the odds.

And here is a plaque with the story of Lena Long, the Traditional Owner of Pierre Spring, with a big smile and a lot of curly white hair in the photo. "It was a holiday place, a break from station work," she said. "I was born close to here, at Well 7.

"Mum went up the Canning Stock Route. She had labour pains one night. She said, 'Must be my baby coming.' And it was me! And she said, 'Gotta get on the horse tomorrow'. Got straight back on the horse. I was in a little carrying bag. I went to Well 7 with her and she said, 'See that tree over there? That was where you were born. That's your hospital over there.'"

Milnyirri was the Aboriginal name for the place. Sir John Forrest, explorer and later Governor of Western Australia, gave the spring its European name in 1874. It was named after Tommy Pierre, an invaluable and respected Indigenous man in Forrest's team.

Hubert Trotman, a member of Canning's survey group recalled that, "It was Tommy Pierre who had been heard to say, 'John Forrest, he very good man, but no good without Tommy Pierre,' which remark might well be said of most explorers and their guides, for if it had not been for our black friends many of those early explorers would have perished."

A dusty ute pulls into the campsite. It is a man past middle age travelling alone. He is criss-crossing the Centre, along the rough tracks. Is he concerned about being on his own?

"I used to be a pilot," he drawls, in an educated accent. "I used to do survey flying for a while, about 15 metres above the ground." If that doesn't scare the daylights out of you, obviously driving these remote tracks alone is not going to worry you. He likes following where the explorers went but, "All that struggle and hardship they went through. If they had just waited 50 years they could have done it all by plane." That's a startling thought.

Three more vehicles pull up for a chat. One of them is a neatly-dressed lady of indeterminate age. She is on her first ever trip camping in the Outback. What a track to choose! Once committed, you can't get off this train for at least three weeks.

She looks as if she is on her way to the RSL club to have a little drink with her friends; her hair is nicely permed and she is wearing makeup and jewellery. She has a sort of startled-deer expression and a wavery smile. "How's it going?" we ask. "Alright, I think," she replies bravely, giving her bracelets a little shake.

MIDNIGHT SPECIAL CAMP: WELL 12

Imagine bringing a mob of cattle down the Canning and arriving at a well with plenty of water from deep underground. The cattle are raging and bellowing with thirst, pushing and shoving around the well. There is a wooden fence around a deep shaft, with its bucket and a pulley, and a long trough to tip the water into. Lovely, lifesaving water for man and beast.

After the track was no longer used for droving (the last mob went through in 1959) the wells started to disintegrate, and most became ruins. Just a hole in the ground, choked with fallen timbers and metal. A lot are still like that.

Then about 15 years ago some of the wells started to be restored, the ones with the best water, anyway. Most of the work has been done by a hardy group of volunteers, TrackCare WA. I would guess they are mostly retired tradies and engineers and their equally practical-looking wives.

The group gets some sponsorship for materials but pay their own way. Some other enthusiasts have also pitched in here and there. We saw a sign from the Chamberlain Tractor Club at Well 5 and there is a toilet construction claimed by the Geraldton 4WD Club at Well 6.

The restorations have been done very sensitively, retaining everything possible. On Well 6 I even found an original tin cup, rusted out and still hanging on a bolt. It had been ingeniously fashioned by some long-gone hand from a tin can with a piece of wire carefully twisted for the handle.

Now every 40 or 50 kilometres along the way you pull up after a long, hot, dusty day and can actually draw the water from the well. Where the shaft is tapped into an artesian well, it is even warm. The deepest is 31 metres (104 feet); drop a pebble and there is a pause before there is a little splash far below. Clean, drinkable water—the pleasures of life reduce to the absolute simplest out here.

In addition to this unexpected luxury, the TrackCare people (why are they all called Bill or Bob?) are constructing long-drop toilets at the campsites. These are ingenious: built off the ground, with the pan mounted on a trolley with a drawbar. There is a polite request inside to (if it's full) attach it to your vehicle, tow it away and empty it into a pit, just follow the signs. "Thank you—Job Done," says the sign. Boom-Boom.

So we are driving along, calling on the two-way radio every now and again to see if anyone else is out there, when we get a response. "Party of eleven vehicles proceeding south." Heading our way, and not far off.

When we pull off in a tiny clear patch beside the track to let them past, we find that they are a TrackCare WA team on their way back from completing a job. Well 18, a day ahead of us, is now restored and the water is good.

"I did my first piece of graffiti ever," I tell one of them. His face clouds. "I wrote Thank You!! beside the TrackCare sticker on Well 12." He laughs and drives off with a wave.

We watch them go past, waving and thanking each car. One woman, with a wrinkled and leathery face and a happy smile, leans out of the driver's window. "It's so much fun and it's so satisfying," she calls out cheerfully.

We push on to well 15 for the night. We know it will be a bit too far but, strangely, in all this almost infinite area of nothing, it is hard to find space in the spinifex to set up camp—spinifex is so spiky and prickly it is miserable to try to camp among it, and it stretches in sheets to the horizon here. But even ruined wells still have a flat cleared space around the hole where you can camp easily, so we aim for that.

It starts to get dark, and in the tropics that happens very fast. One minute it is broad daylight and then suddenly the sun has set in a blaze of red, dropped below the horizon, and a black sky is filled with stars. It's very beautiful, but driving is a bit tricky with just a rough barely-defined track to follow. There isn't much alternative at this point, though, and we plough on. Almost there.

Then, one kilometre out we have a sand dune moment. We fail to make it over the crest and are bogged, right on the top. It is a truth that given a sand dune to bog in, the moment will always be inconvenient. It is also true that this time it is a bit predictable. The sand dries out all morning and it is best not to be trying to cross a dune after about mid-afternoon.

We all stand around it, pondering what to do. I think there is a pretty even chance we will be spending the night there, perched on the top of the hill, with the car pointing downwards on one side, and the camper pointing downwards on the other. We do a bit of exploratory poking around the wheels, but the sand is too soft and deep. We are not going to get out of there on our own.

So we dig the snatch strap out of the recovery box. It is a long strip of webbing that can be attached between two vehicles for towing. Hang a weight on it, to stop it flinging back and killing someone if it snaps, and stand well back. Stuart and Nonie's car in front gives a steady heave, and we are over.

By then it is very dark, but we pick out the well by reading the GPS coordinates and are beamed in. Another campfire, another restored well (Thank You!!) a clear space to camp and it is home for the night.

Murray Rankin's Trolley Camp: Well 15

If you've got a lazy year or so, and are really, really sick of your current lifestyle, you could do what Murray Rankin did. He set off with a mate, John Foulsham, to walk the length of the Canning from the south.

"In Easter 1971 we went up to Wiluna and we saw the Canning Stock Route on the map," John remembers. "It was one of those maps that showed a great big line and it looked like a highway through the desert.

"And we said, 'That's interesting, we should walk that.'" Interesting indeed!

They set off but had to turn back when it became obvious that the plan needed quite a bit of fine-tuning, like building a hand-pulled trailer that you could actually get over sand hills, for instance.

In 1972 Rankin set off again with two English brothers, Peter and John Waterfall. (It is hard to imagine a surname more out of place than waterfall in this region.) The equipment was still the big problem—how to carry supplies for a walk of three months or more in that terrain. The trolley they were dragging, this time just a light metal frame with a couple of pushbike wheels, is still sitting beside the track near Well 15 where they, unsurprisingly, abandoned the attempt.

Undeterred, in 1976 Murray Rankin found another three hardy, or more accurately, foolhardy, friends willing to accompany him for another go. They set out from Halls Creek and actually, finally walked—walked!—all the way from Halls Creek in the north to Wiluna in the south. Walked! (I know I'm repeating myself, but…walked!). That's 2000 kilometres, on foot, through this incredibly harsh, unforgiving region. Unbelievable!

I think that's enough exclamation marks for now. Let's talk about the serious matter of keeping clean. This is what you need to know about doing your washing on the Canning:

1. Don't bother—red dust suits most complexions.

2. When washing, expect the water to be about the colour of the landscape. You will smell better but your clothes will soon match everything else.

3. If you are washing in a creek, don't look too closely at the water.

4. If you are washing at a well, be grateful that you just have to pull the water up with a bucket and a pulley. Think of your sisters in the third world, walking miles a day with a big pot of water on their heads.

5. Then drop your bucket in. Try not to let go of the string. If you do, swear, stand with your hands on your hips for a while watching it circling gently in the middle, trailing its string. Then go and fetch a spanner, unscrew your sand flag from the bumper bar of the car and fish it out.

6. Then sit on a folding stool, get a couple of basins of water and try to make the clothes a bit better than they were before.

7. Don't worry—everyone else looks the same.

Durba Springs: Near Well 17

What's that? I can't hear the peace and quiet over the noise of the generator and the dirt bikes.

Remember the blokes back at Wiluna? The ones with the four dirt bikes and the trailer full of spare tyres, parts, 44-gallon drums of fuel, gas bottles and tents? We were pretty sure we would encounter them again along the way and we expected that they would be a rowdy lot, drinking and mucking around and generally disturbing the peace.

Sure enough we had been nicely set up at our first camp at Pierre Spring when they rolled, or rather roared, into the campsite. We can't really complain, after all they had personally given us the hint that this was a great spot to camp.

They had been very friendly and easy-going and had given us some good ideas about quite a few nice places to stay along the way. Pity about the generator in the quiet of the evening, but what can you do?

But by now we know that they are really nice blokes just out to have a good time. A couple of cousins, a couple of their sons and nephews. Not at all the lairs and boofheads we had expected.

Next time we meet up with them is at here at Durba Springs, another one of their recommendations. This is a gorgeous place to stay. There is a circle of rust-red cliffs rising around a pool of water. The ground is grassy. Grassy! Yes! Actually soft underfoot. There are fire-pits, built by the Indigenous rangers, and the TrackCare WA angels have put in a long-drop toilet.

After a hard, hot day of rough track it is like a true oasis. And a popular one; everyone stops here and usually seems to stay a couple of nights. It could have been named for a Durbar—that was a get-together in Imperial India. But actually it comes from the Aboriginal name, Jirrpa.

This evidently has a long history as a stopping place for Europeans. On the rock wall at the edge of the pond are a handful of names and dates carved into the stone. There is nothing recent. The oldest, "Bull", in precise copperplate, is dated 1906. His name is not on the list of the first survey party of six men who travelled through that year, so we wonder who was Mr Bull who had such very neat handwriting, even on stone?

The Dirt Bike Boys have their tents set up when we arrive and are sitting in a circle around their campfire. There is also a noisy group of Norwegians laughing in another part of the grassy space. The RSL club lady's group is camped at the far end; she wanders over for a chat. "How's it going?" we ask tentatively. "Not bad, better than I expected," she replies bravely, patting her hairdo as if to reassure herself that it is still there.

How do you come to love the noise of a generator? When there is a charging problem with Nonie and Stuart's vehicle and those blokes enthusiastically lend it to us to help us work out what is wrong. Ah, sweet music to the ears. These are very nice guys. It turns out they are part of a Greek family that owns the biggest fruit and vegetable wholesaling business in Australia. This explains why the ute's number plate is TOMATO.

There's a few bucks in greens obviously. They have all the best equipment: top of the line tents, a 60-litre freezer, a shower system, the four dirt bikes, that generator. Their satellite phone is in constant use, hang the expense. And—here's the real kicker—one of the cars is shrink wrapped. Yep, every panel has been covered in plastic to protect it from scratches from the shrubs beside the track. "Hey, Yianni, shrink wrap me car will ya? I'm going to the desert."

They are also having a Boys Own Adventure good time, roaring around on the bikes and tinkering with them. And eating hot dogs; we were presented with one, wrapped in a slab of white bread and tomato sauce, when we wandered over to have a chat.

That would be the first one I have eaten for at least 20 years. Takes you back, really, and makes a nice retro match with the individually-wrapped, processed cheddar cheese slices, straight out of our childhoods, that Nonie accidentally bought, and we are now having for lunch every day until they are gone, hearing our mothers' voices saying, "Waste not, want not," in our ears as we dutifully munch away.

The clearing here at Durba Springs opens out into a little gorge with the dry, rocky bed of a creek in the middle. It must rain here sometimes, to create this. It would be spectacular seeing the water roaring through. It would also be spectacular seeing one of those huge red rocks break away from the cliff and come crashing down.

The edges are lined with massive boulders that have done just that. It would undoubtedly be your last sight. We take a walk along, looking for the Aboriginal Art that is said to be here, and sit eating a biscuit, looking thoughtfully at those boulders piled all around us and hoping that it isn't our unlucky day.

We don't find the Aboriginal rock paintings, but all along the way we are entranced by the tiny natural works of art: lizards and bugs perfectly camouflaged. A yellow and black insect on the one yellow and black rock, a red and black one on a perfectly matched stone, a lizard with its orange back the colour of the sand. Fabulous. You'd think they planned it that way.

Back at Wiluna we had heard that Connie Sue Beadell, so famous to us from the Anne Beadell Highway and the Connie Sue Highway, was leading a tag-along group travelling south to end up at Wiluna, and we really hoped that we would meet her.

After doing some back-of-the-envelope calculations, we had estimated that we might coincide here on the same night, and late in the afternoon a clutch of dusty 4WDs drive into the campsite, following a twin-cab Land Rover Defender that looks like a desert warrior.

Len Beadell wrote several memoirs about his life out in the bush. They show that he had a great sense of humour and a talent for drawing cartoons. We had found them at Laverton and Stuart bought the whole set, packaged in a box that looks like a dunny (the traditional Australian outhouse where you can sit with the door open and commune with nature while you commune with nature). Stuart tucks one of the books in his pocket and we wander over.

Connie Sue is sitting in a camp chair that has seen a lot of Outback life, filling in the log for the day on her laptop. She looks up with a smile. Her hair is cut in a blunt bob and she is dressed in a khaki t-shirt and a pair of roomy shorts. Her husband Mick is entering fuel consumption figures into a complicated-looking spreadsheet. His battered and sweat-stained Akubra hat has lived a harder life even than the camp chair.

Connie Sue signs Stuart's book and politely passes the time of day. They have been on the road now for three weeks leading the group and are close to the end, but she seems very relaxed; this part of the world has always been her playground and her home.

Mick is a man of few words and the ones he allows to escape are, country-style, blunt and discouraging. We don't blame him. Leading groups of clueless tourists would make anyone morose, and he undoubtedly thinks we are just as gormless.

Did I see his lip curl when we said we are towing camper trailers? I think so but, to be fair, we have already seen two sad broken trailers abandoned beside the track.

"Yer got it all ahead of yer," he says sourly, not making eye contact. "You'll be wonderin' why you ever set out when yer get halfway up the track."

We take a breath and, to lift the tone, prattle on brightly, telling him we had owned an old Defender, and had driven it from England to Australia in 1972.

"Yer musta had rocks in yer head," he mutters, not looking up, and in a dismal farewell, "good luck, youse'll need it."

But, among the doom and gloom, he lets out some valuable tips about how to read a sand dune to increase the chances of getting over in one attempt. And—it feels very special that after roaming around these parts and coming across her family's story and her own name in so many places—we got to meet Connie Sue in person.

Lake Disappointment Heights Camp: Near Well 20

Prestige waterfront setting! Looking out across this spectacular lake, you would swear that just beyond the dunes on the other side there is a surf beach.

But if you set off with your beach towel over your shoulder you are in for a big surprise. And a big disappointment. On this side of the dunes there is just a huge, crusty salt lake without a drop of water, and on the other side you've got several thousand kilometres to trudge before you can dive in to the surf.

But it is a lovely place to camp with those beautiful misleading views of not-water. And there is enough cloud in the sky to give a sensational gold and silver sunset splashing the sky and reflecting off the salt lake.

Just before Lake Disappointment (and we feel so sorry for the explorers, just imagine their excited first sight of that glistening lake and the crushing disappointment to find it was nothing but dry salt) there is a stream that drains to it, Savory Springs. This has actual water, quite a lot of it. Nonie bounds down to the waters' edge to taste it. Aargh! Phht! It is indeed as extremely salty as the map says.

We all sit watching the sunset display from our home at Lake Disappointment Heights (Nonie and Stuart's camper is lower on the slope—Lake Disappointment Flats) and talk about the day. We are, day by day, getting a lot further north. We have crossed the Tropic of Capricorn and are now about the same latitude as Rockhampton and Longreach. The days are getting warmer and the sunrises and sunsets are getting more and more extravagant.

Pit Bull Camp: Well 24

Pit Bull Camp was a late contender for the name of today's camp, but it came through like Stephen Bradbury on the ice at the 2002 Winter Olympics, to be a clear winner.

44-Gallon Camp had been leading the field until then as the most likely title. Way back when we were planning this trek, we worked out that we would not have enough fuel to get to the next possible place to fill up, at Kunawarritji Aboriginal Community, about half way along the route.

What people do instead is to order a 44-gallon (200 litre) drum of fuel to be left at a fuel dump along the way. Darren (of course he's called Darren) comes out from Newman, 600 kilometres to the west, with a load of drums, sets them down beside the track here, writes the names on them with felt pen and leaves them to their fate.

It is $3 a litre, it is paid in advance—$600—and you just take your chances and hope that no-one has knocked off your fuel before you get to it. But there is no alternative. What else are you going to do?

Because, of course, it is really, really remote here. How can I convey to you just how remote? Try this: imagine the map of Australia. Think about a spot in the very middle. That's Alice Springs with Uluru (the massive monolith of red stone that used to be called Ayers Rock) nearby. Now draw a smudgy circle a bit to the north-west of Alice. That's the Little Sandy Desert. The Canning Stock Route is a skinny line snaking its way up the Little Sandy Desert all the way from the Great Victoria Desert in the south to the Tanami Desert in the north.

It is just a spidery line across absolutely nothing. Alfred Canning must have been an extraordinary bloke, working for two years in these truly trackless wastes, trudging along, putting in a well about every 20 miles. It's just the same as in the Middle East, where the caravanserais were about the same distance apart, a day's trek for a camel train.

But just because it is isolated, and a desert, don't imagine for a moment that there is no scenery out here. That's another challenge—how to describe the fantastic, fascinating panorama that unfolds every day.

Ok, here goes:

The first surprise is that it is completely different to the Lawrence of Arabia image from the movies. It is not sweeping, knife-edged sand dunes with nothing but ripples and shadows on them. In these deserts the scenery changes every few hundred metres.

There is a huge variety of desert vegetation, mostly of course scrubby, hardy, woody, prickly plants, but they grow in patches. Now there will be a sweep of waist-high bushes with flat tops and khaki-coloured leaves, filling the whole space between two sand dunes.

Then, abruptly it is replaced by something knee-high and of a completely different green. Bushy, brushy, spiky, fluffy, shiny, stiff and erect or waving in the breeze, it's all out there but in big swathes, like the plantings they used to do in the spreading English aristocratic estates.

At this time of year, the spinifex (all ten varieties of it) is blooming, and the tiny, creamy flowers look just like a field of wheat, filling the view until there is an abrupt change and another plant takes the stage.

And the dunes, long parallel lines of ochre-red ridges, are studded with bushes all over them, in shades of green from ashy grey to kelly green, and with the bare orange-coloured earth a dramatic contrast in between them. They are stunning.

There are patches of scruffy mulga and stands of stark white snow gums. There are desert poplars, innocent-looking little trees that are tyre killers—they throw down dead branches that have murderous spikes that can stab a tyre with ease.

And there are desert oaks that stand in lines like a little bit of Tuscany except that here there is no olive grove and no medieval stone farmhouse.

Of all this breathtaking plant life we have been enchanted in particular by one, the Holly Grevillea. This delicate, graceful little tree, with its clusters of tiny red bells and its spiked leaves just like an English holly bush, keeps making an appearance, and it is always a star.

Then, of course, there is a backdrop to all the bushes, which also changes all the time. A series of sand dunes stretching away, one after another. Or a flat, stony wasteland covered in shiny brown gibbers the size of a man's fist. A wide plain like the savannah grasslands of Africa, and with trees just like the signature flat-topped African trees, but only waist-high. Or rolling sandy wastes with massive outcrops of red-rock ranges in the distance.

Now this is all very poetic but I'm sure what you really want to know is why this is called Pit Bull Camp.

There is not much wildlife to be seen out here. There is an occasional wallaby, so there must be some very sparse mobs of them, but it is a rare sighting. There are quite a lot of feral camels stalking around looking disdainful, with their noses in the air. There are some birds of course, mainly small, fast ones zipping around here and there.

And there are lizards, apparently some very large ones by the look of their tracks in the sand, but we have not seen any of those. Most of the animals who live out here are small, scurrying things that come out at night. And of course, the snakes who prey on them.

And then there are the dingoes. These native dogs are the kings of the country, and they know it. They will stand by the side of the track, arrogantly watching you pass. They will walk down the track towards the car, playing chicken, then step neatly away into the bush at the last moment casting a scornful look back at you.

When we pull into camp there is a dingo sniffing around. It is not a very nice campsite, but there isn't any choice. It has an acceptable flat clear space, but the well is in ruins except for a puddle of slimy green water in the hole. There is dung all around—camel, wallaby, and smaller creatures.

The dingo takes its time checking to see what he can find, and after having a good look he trots away into the bush, with a last baleful glance back. We have a great meal, as usual, and settle down for a pleasant evening. As the indigo dark of the night falls a dingo starts howling somewhere nearby, that eerie, mournful cry. Then another answers, from somewhere else, and another, building louder and louder.

About 3.00 am we are woken by a full-on dogfight just beside our camper, a frenzy of yelping and barking. When we look outside there are four dingoes, three going hell for leather, one running around the outside of the brawling mass, leaping up and down in excitement. It is a melee of biting, barking ferocity. Ren shines his torch and shouts at them. He would have liked to throw a bucket of water on them but considering we are actually in a desert, he didn't want to waste the water.

But they get the message, or one of them triumphs, because they give up and vanish back into the bush, leaving Nonie and Stuart to make jokes about neighbours who can't control their pets.

Full Moon Camp: Well 21

If it doesn't say restored on the map, the well is always in ruins. The structure has collapsed and there is just a hole with some rusty metal and broken beams. Sometimes there is water, murky brown or green and covered with flies and insects. Sometimes the earth has fallen in and it is dry. And (I really like this) there is usually the rusty remains of one of the original sturdy buckets, now over a hundred years old.

Those buckets are beautiful in an industrial-art kind of way. Tall, cylindrical, with a solid, pleasingly curved handle and a strip of iron forming a collar around the top. Absolutely fit for purpose, and so heavy I can hardly lift them off the ground, let alone drag them up full of water.

There are new ones in the same style at some of the restored wells, made of stainless steel. Maybe they will last 100 years. The restorations look as if they might, at least, and the TrackCare motto is "Access for the Future."

Anyway, we are at an unrestored well tonight, but it is a clean, clear space with no litter. (It is amazing how much travellers care for these campsites; there is never a scrap of rubbish.)

We spend half the evening trying to decide if it is full moon (party animals that we are) and the other half listening to a podcast of Thank God it's Friday, out in the middle of nowhere, with the volume cranked up and no-one to annoy except the wildlife.

The moonlight is too bright to have the full big-bowl-of-stars night sky that the Outback specialises in, but the evening star looks very red, the moon looks very white and as usual we can see the Southern Cross, our Southern Cross, that always, every night, makes my heart skip a beat.

Fly Camp: Well 31

All along we have been saying, "Where are the flies?" Our Outback adventures in the past have been dogged by bush flies. Not the sort of disgusting, enormous city blowflies that are so big they leave footprints on you and could probably rip your arm off if they really tried.

No, Outback flies are little pesky, get-under-your-fly-veil flies. More persistent than a four-year-old's questions. More irritating than an election advertisement. More annoying than a leaf blower. They can drive you crazy in a flash, crawling all over you, trying to get into your ears and your nose, leaving you swinging and swatting in a futile attempt to get them to leave.

But strangely, this trip there have been no flies. Until today. All that about these infuriating crazy-making flies—yes, that has been our afternoon. Cup of tea? Drink it under the veil. Glass of wine? Under the veil. Go for a run? Put on the joggers, the hi-tech running shorts, the Nike running top, the iPhone-holding armband, the headphones, the cap. And the fly veil.

Yep, now that's a good look. Fortunately, there is no-one to see it except our little group and what goes on trek stays on trek. This was a good run, though, following the footsteps of a dingo. Hang on, what did I just say? Yes, but it felt safe; after all there was no Death Adder soft sand on this track today. Everything's relative.

Just for example, how about those massive, ferocious-looking black and yellow hornets that arrive as soon as we try to take a shower today. They are like something out of a cartoon—far too colourful and too big and too loud to be real, they zoom towards the basin of water (and you) in a Spitfire squadron formation, ready to attack. Disney eat your heart out.

And then, sitting waiting for dinner, I see firstly a pencil-thin baby brown snake slither past my toes, then frantically try to escape from me and hide in a clump of spinifex by rearing up and lying very still against it. Just after that a scorpion trots nonchalantly past me in front of the camp fire.

And yes, it wasn't full moon last night, it is full moon tonight...we think.

Halfway Camp: Well 35

We've made it to halfway! Wiluna is 1100 kilometres behind us, far to the south and Halls Creek is 950 ahead.

Glancing off to each side, Port Hedland is way over there on the coast 750 kilometres to the west and Alice Springs is 1100 kilometres to the east. We sure are a long way from anywhere.

Right at this most central point is an Aboriginal Community, Kunawarritji. We hoped to top up with diesel and a few supplies at the store, but it is impossible to know what these communities will be like until you get there. One thing you can be sure of: the fuel will be heart-stoppingly expensive and so will the few measly items available at the shop—jars of strawberry jam, packets of cornflakes and a freezer full of sliced white bread.

There is no-one at the fuel shed when we get there, and the pumps have padlocks on them. So we go in search of someone to sell us some diesel. There are a few dusty buildings dotted around and a gate barring our entry to the community residential area. There is one Indigenous woman stirring something behind a door and we poke our head in.

"She over there, in the clinic," says the shy dark-skinned woman, nodding across the path. We walk over, knock, look around inside.

"Oh, hello," says a chirpy European woman with a broad Scots accent. She is wearing large shirt with a vivid Aboriginal art pattern. "She's just gone over to clean the motel units." Just across the way are half a dozen actual little motel rooms made out of corrugated iron. A tired-looking blonde is wielding a mop.

"Sorry, no-one was around so I thought I'd just go over and do the rooms," she says, plodding back to the store. She has been there four years with her partner Tas, the CEO.

When we meet him, he is full of enthusiasm for his job, the people, the place and his plans for the future of the community. He is improving the houses, making a new football field, organising a Battle of the Bands competition.

Despite the appearances, this desolate-looking little cluster of buildings in the middle of nowhere makes a healthy half million a year, mostly from travellers passing through, buying fuel at $3.40 a litre, picking up essentials at the little shop and, recently, staying at the new set of motel rooms, or even just taking a hot shower at $10 a go.

We are just at the start of the season for travellers passing through. It is much too hot in summer. The temperature reaches upward of 50 degrees Celsius (122 degrees Fahrenheit) so it is too dangerous to attempt to travel the track until about now. The trickle of 4WD tourists out for a bit of adventure builds up from May, doing the Canning or travelling east-west through from Alice to the coast. By July they will be lined up for fuel two deep right back to the road, a hundred metres back. Ker-ching.

We buy a couple of things, I do a load of washing ($5) and we ask Tas about himself. "I used to be a musician. I was an impersonator, I used to do Johnny Cash, Crowded House, Charlie Rich," he says. He is ticking them off on his fingers as he speaks and tallies up ten or twelve. "I worked all over." In Sydney? Where? "Lots of places, like the Harbord Diggers Club."

There does seem something of the ageing musician about Tas, once he tells us this. He is certainly friendly, personable and energetic. Kunawaritji is lucky to have found him and made him fall in love with it. But why, we do wonder, is a white couple running this place, why not an Indigenous family? We don't know the answer, but we keep wondering this a lot out here.

There are hardly any people around. There have been three deaths lately and most of the community is away on "sorry business", the Aboriginal term for funerals. One was a murder right here; a woman stabbed her husband and he died of his wounds.

The local Indigenous people have native title to a vast area of land around this community. There is little employment. A few are rangers, but most people live on welfare. They sometimes still go out and spend time in the wild, camping and hunting.

Some of the older people still know the traditional bush skills, like tracking; one elderly lady with Alzheimers wandered off and her son found her. He followed her tracks out into the bush, firstly from his car, then on foot, and brought her home a few hours later. It's hard to know what will happen when this generation dies out. The young have few skills, few opportunities and hardly anything to do to fill in the days. The Battle of the Bands sounds like a great idea.

Near the community is a well with a real windmill, turning lazily in the breeze. Around the rusty stand there is lush grass, a few square metres of it, a splash of vivid green in the red dirt. We have lunch, reminisce about where we have been so far and then head off again, striking out for the second half of the trek.

A couple of kilometres along the way there is a Landcruiser, pulled up at the side of the road. A wiry bloke with a battered Akubra hat is standing by it, holding a beer. "Smoko," he calls out as we pull up, waving the bottle in greeting. "G'day, me name's Brian." We settle in for a yarn. His shirt is branded with the Noccundrah Pub, near Thargomindah in far Western Queensland. He comes from out that way and is keen to talk about it.

Thargomindah is a little place and, like so many of the small towns, has only one police officer serving a gigantic area. It's a lovely job when things are going well, with just a few minor infringements and a bit of advice to the local lads, but if there is a serious problem, he is on his own with no backup for hours or even days. We've heard about this before—the problem of how to administer vast areas, with the lone police officer left to deal with it all as best he can.

The conversation turns to the weather, of course, and the likelihood of rain and he tells us about one wet spell.

"So there had been a load of rain this time," he says. "And it led to me sort of makin' an arrest. The road was cut, and this young bloke comes roarin' through, ignores the Road Closed sign and keeps goin'. Next day he's back, on foot. He's got bogged 48 kilometres out there and walked back.

So, we go out with him and his 4WD isn't just bogged, it's buried, up to the door sills. We take him back to town with us. There's something a bit suss about him, he's very vague on details about himself, and just something makes me wonder, so I had taken note of the number plate.

Meanwhile I give me mate Vaughan, the copper at Thargo, a call and sure enough it turns out the vehicle is stolen, and the bloke has quite a few warrants out for him: drive-off from service stations, theft, armed robbery. A cop nearly got him not long ago and the bloke injured the cop's arm gettin' away, so they were seriously after him.

'Can you hang onto him?' Vaughan asks. 'I'm tied up here and can't get there for a few hours.' So, when we get back we take him to the pub, acting very friendly, give him a couple of drinks and dinner and put him up in a room for the night. The publican's in on it too.

After all of that he's sleepin' sweetly in the bedroom in the pub, not suspectin' a thing and the cop arrives, opens the door with the key and he's got the handcuffs on him before he's even awake."

Brian gives a wheezy laugh and shakes his head at the memory.

We wave goodbye and we're on our way again. It's just more bone-jarring, teeth-rattling corrugations and another well, until it's time to stop for the day. I look at my phone. It says, "You have no scheduled events for tomorrow." Too true, just the way we want it.

Desert Oak Camp: Just past Well 39

So far, despite punishing corrugations, chopped-away washouts, rocky outcrops, and challenging sand dunes, our vehicles have kept running. Stuart and Nonie have trashed one tyre, when a piece of wood staked a wheel from the side.

It is so tempting, when you have juddered along on those murderous corrugations for what seems like forever, to move just a little bit sideways, to slip up onto the smooth edge of the road, beside the bushes, with your left-hand wheels out of the corrugations. Aah, so sweet.

But danger lurks there: sticks embedded in the sand and almost invisible. That is what happened to Nonie and Stuart's tyre. I could hear the conversation as clearly as if I had been in the car with them:

Driver: "I'm fed up with these corrugations, I'm going to go up onto the smooth for a bit."

Passenger: "That's not a good idea, you could easily puncture a tyre."
Driver: "Don't be silly, that won't happen."
Passenger: "You're making a mistake, it could really cost us."
Driver: "Don't be ridiculous, I'm just pulling to the side a bit…Oops."

I think we should draw a veil over the conversation that probably followed, don't you?

But apart from this there haven't been any issues, no flat tyres, no mechanical problems. We haven't needed to call Andy, thank goodness. "4WD rescue and recovery, no location too remote," Andy declares confidently. He has marked his territory in lots of places along the way before we even got to the Canning. Any notice board has a fly-specked business card pinned crookedly to it, any shelter shed has his details hand written in permanent marker on one of the beams.

We would definitely like to meet Andy, he's probably quite a character, but we would like to meet him over a beer, not in the way he would like to meet us, loading our vehicle onto his super-tough 4WD go-anywhere breakdown recovery truck.

We are learning a few new skills: how to read a dune as we approach it, by the shape of the wheel tracks on it; how to spot the next well, by the little cluster of lush trees around it; how to ride the corrugations, when to skip across them and when to crawl.

Mostly we get a really good look at the scenery as we go along, because we usually choose to crawl. We really, really don't want to break something and have to call Andy. Even to think about what he would charge to come and rescue us makes our eyes water.

So, we average less than 20 kilometres an hour; 100 kilometres a day is a good day's drive. On one long slow stretch of corrugations Ren said, "Going this slowly, I reckon I could get out and walk beside the car, if I just tied a bit of string to the steering wheel." We laugh, but it does remind us of a train trip we did in the Sudan long ago, where people actually did get out and walk beside the train.

We stop on and off during the day to air up and air down. When the dunes are soft, you lower your tyre pressure to around 20 psi, or even less sometimes. It gives a wider footprint to walk over the soft sand and not sink in. When the track is rocky or hard, though, you can easily get a puncture with that very low tyre pressure.

So, every day we are letting air out or putting it back, sometimes more than once. We each have an air compressor mounted in the engine bay so we can easily pump our tyres up. And here's a little hint: when you crouch down beside the wheel out here, ready to attach the air line, check behind you for any patches of needle-sharp spinifex before lowering your backside.

As we go along the track, we keep in touch with anyone in the vicinity. Everyone is on Channel 40, so every now and again we hear, "Party of 3 vehicles leaving Well 25, travelling north." "Party of two vehicles, got a visual on you." Today we heard, "Young bloke on a solar powered bike travelling south. We just passed him, you might want to give him an orange or something." Yes, I think so.

Everyone stops to say hello as you pass by, asking, "How are you going? How's the track? How many days has it taken you?" It almost always requires manoeuvring for one vehicle to get off and let the other pass, but no-one would dream of driving by without a chat anyway. And strung out across this long, long track of more than 2,000 kilometres, these cars are just a few little dots in a truly gigantic area.

When there is no-one around to be annoyed by it, which is most of the time, we talk to each other on the two-way, usually exclaiming over the scenery. We also give each other a heads-up for tricky bits of the track, as the lead vehicle goes over the sand dunes.

"Rough and bumpy with a soft patch right at the top."

"Bit of a whoopty-do on the other side."

"It's a dromedary."

"Give it some herbs."

"If it rock'n'rolled any more Elvis would come and put it to music."

We both sport jaunty sand flags, waving high in the air. It is de rigeur for vehicles out here. No-one wants to come face-to-face with an oncoming car at the top of a sand hill. So that orange flag, high overhead, gives early warning.

Every 30 kilometres or so from start to finish of the track there is another well, restored or in ruins. We always stop to have a look. There is a tall tripod structure over Well 36, and an old wire gate has been laid across the opening to the shaft. When we look in, the water seems good and not far down.

"Next well to be restored, I think," declares Nonie confidently.

"Yes," I agree, nodding sagely, "I suppose they put that gate over it to stop the animals from fouling it."

We are so very wrong. The tripod was erected to heave a dead camel out of the well, and the gate is there to stop anyone drinking the lethally contaminated water. Oh well, so much for our bushcraft.

About lunchtime today we come to a couple of graves at Well 37. One is marked S&T RIP, the letters made by holes punched into a little square of metal on a post. There is a bit of rough fence around the grave. Next to it is another, just marked "Chinaman." Shoesmith and Thompson were the S & T and Chinaman was an Aboriginal stockman. There were so many violent deaths over time at this well that it came to be known as "The Haunted Well."

About 20 people are standing around having a look at the graves. They are a tag-along group travelling south, with nine vehicles. They look very enthusiastic and as they are only five days in, still clean and fresh. They are all grey nomads, cheerful retirees having a great time.

It was dangerous to be out here in those early days, 100 years ago. At Well 40 there is a grave for Michael Tobin. He and his brother were on Canning's team. He was speared here, got off a shot that killed his assailant, but died himself. There is a solid headstone marking his final resting place. It seems such a lonely place to lie.

The landscape is changing, getting even harsher. There are long bare swales between the dunes and the rocky outcrops are getting bigger and bolder. There is a beautiful little gorge, the Wardabunna Rockhole, with deep, cool water that would almost tempt you to take a dip, if it wasn't for all the camel dung around it.

We put a few more dunes behind us then we stop to camp in a grove of desert oaks, the comical mop top casuarina trees. Tomorrow, first thing, there is a lake to cross, and not just a crust of salt this time. It has rained here in the last few days, and we were told today that it is still very muddy.

Boiling Billy Camp: Well 42

It would be very different travelling solo. The four of us are very communal, eating together, talking on and off all day on the two-way radio, sitting together by the campfire. Sometimes we play Scrabble. Nonie brought Pictionary. Stuart is going to teach us some card games. Mostly, though, we just sit and chat companionably.

But the Outback is scattered with men travelling alone. The very remoteness attracts eccentrics and interesting characters. Everyone is happy to talk but it is strictly first-names only. Some of the men are undoubtedly running away from something: a relationship gone sour, a bit of bother, financial troubles.

But a lot are just single and doing their thing, or they have a wife who doesn't like this sort of travel and happily waves them off for a while. A bloke alone can have some unexpected experiences.

Back at Kunawarritjiri Brian had told us about one time when he was out on the road:

"I was deliverin' a load of cattle so I couldn't have a drink, but I went into a pub just for a coffee. I had a bit of a yarn with the barman, then went on me way.

"The next night I was comin' back the opposite direction and went in again. There was a tribe of backpackers sittin' around and I start to have a few jokes with them.

"Then the barman calls out from a back room, 'Is that you Brian, can you serve behind the bar for a bit, I'm busy out here?'

"I'd only met him the night before, but no worries. I go behind the bar. 'How do you open the till?' I call out.

'It's the button that's nearly worn out,' he calls back.

So I pull beers for a coupla hours. Never met 'im before and never seen 'im again."

A lot of these solitary men are like Pete. He has set up camp at Well 42 when we arrive. We knew he was out there, we saw him once driving past a place where we were having lunch, but he just gave a wave then and he doesn't come over the two-way at all.

When we are set up we go over to say g'day. He's very friendly and happy to talk. His wife doesn't like to rough it, he tells us, and he's got a caravan to go with her on more sedate holidays, but he likes this wilder stuff. So, he's doing it alone and will meet up with a mate somewhere east of Kununurra to continue on with a blokey fishing kind of holiday.

There are, of course, hazards to travelling alone. If you get into trouble, no-one would find you for quite a while, and even with a sat phone you could cark it before help arrives. You can actually die out here, from any number of things: snakebite, car accident, sudden illness. And you can injure yourself in a lot more ways than that.

How about this nasty moment: Pete had been boiling a billy on the gas ring the day before. He reached up and bumped a light, which fell down and knocked the billy over. It was full of boiling water which cascaded down his leg. He was alone. You don't call the Flying Doctor for a burn, but it was a bad one. What to do? He had a little freezer chest, so he grabbed a couple of frozen lamb shanks and tied them onto his leg over the worst spot. First Aid Outback-style.

And in the arena of accidents, every well is the stuff that Occupational Health and Safety nightmares are made of. The winch handle spins around, knocks you on the head, the heavy bucket swings and trips you up and whoopsy, you're in that well with a broken leg or a fractured skull. And there's no ladder.

Amazing that any of us survive, really, and keep coming back for more.

Moet Camp: Well 46

Remember the young bloke with the solar-powered motor bike? The one who might like to have an orange? Halfway along a wide swale between dunes we meet up with him. He is standing beside a truly unique vehicle, one that he built himself. There is a rugged bicycle frame, with chunky bike tyres, and a sturdy-looking trailer unit sporting a rakish bank of solar panels. It is a weird effect, a little bit Mad Max, a little bit Moon Buggy.

The owner of this startling piece of equipment is a slight, softly-spoken young man, Sam Mitchell. His clothes are ragged and dirty, his hair is long, and he hasn't had a shower for rather a long time, but he has a sweet smile and an amazingly relaxed manner for someone who is ever so slowly making his way along the Canning, including the laborious business of getting his ungainly bike over the dunes, which can be long, rough and steep, sometimes all at once.

I don't know how he makes any progress at all, actually, as everyone who passes must stop and talk to him for a long time, asking him all about his strange and fascinating adventure. We do the same, take the photos, ask the questions.

"Leave you with a couple of oranges?" I offer.

"Wouldn't say no to an orange," he replies.

I forage for some more supplies in the lunch box.

"Do you eat cheese?" He flashes another of his engaging smiles. Nonie has been mining their food box too and is handing over muesli bars.

"Coke?" I venture hesitantly, holding out a cold one. He gives a happy little in-draw of breath as he reaches for it.

We drive off, wondering if he will make it, or if his bike will die a sad death and end up abandoned beside the track, like Murray Rankin's trolley, to become part of the legend of the Canning.

Well 41 is supposed to have been restored but when we get there we don't even take emergency water out. The well does have water in it, but it looks very unappetising. The timbers are all broken and there is no bucket or pulley. And there is a smelly little pond next to it, muddy, grey and edged with camel dung. It is disappointing, we had planned to wash our clothes and our hair, and had imagined pouring buckets of cold, fresh water over us.

Then Well 42 is a stinking hole with a puddle in the bottom, coated with a thick film and buzzing with insects. There are just a couple of bits of broken wood and rusted tin lying in the shaft from the original structure.

The volunteer restoration teams are working on the wells with the best water, and it is not so crucial to survival these days to have them at the old 20-mile intervals, so many of these sad old wells are destined to remain derelict. We push on.

Remember Lake Disappointment? The one that was just a dry crust of salt? There is another not-lake straight after Well 42. Instead of water, Gulli Lake is covered with the fashion food of the moment. In the big cities, so Nonie tells me, foam and jus have given way to the current fad for samphire. Apparently it costs a packet down there in restaurant-land, but up here it grows wild in sheets sweeping across the flat plains. It is a small succulent, sometimes a delicate green and sometimes red-tinged.

We nibble a bit. It is crunchy, juicy and salty, rather nice. We imagine how much we are saving by eating it right here, for nothing, and what buckets of money we could make if we could just get it down to the coast. Oh well, I guess we're not destined to make our fortunes that way.

There is a little plaque at Well 46. The restoration has been dedicated to the grandson of Alfred Canning. Peter Canning visited the stock route each year from 1974-9, until he got too old, in tribute to his grandfather. We can understand. It was dreadful for the First Nations people and their treatment was unforgiveable but, nevertheless, the further we travel along this route the more we admire the incredible effort and determination that was required for Alfred Canning to get out here and keep going, sinking these wells and overcoming immense obstacles and hardship in the process.

When we stop for the night, Darryl and Leanne pull in to camp at the same site. We have met them along the way over the last couple of days, and they say they have laughed at Nonie and me rabbiting on over the two-way without knowing they are there, listening in. Nonie and I look at each other, startled.

Darryl and Leanne are easy-going country people from Murwillumbah, on the far north coast of New South Wales. Sydney? "I've been there once," says Darryl. They are entirely happy living on 25 acres, five minutes from work and with plenty of space for their dogs and Leanne's horses.

"Come and have a look at Woolloomooloo, in the middle of Sydney, where we live," I tease him. "Get a look at a slice of life there, surrounded by the druggies and deros." He gives me a pitying smile and shakes his head.

They are spending their long-service leave by loading themselves and their two Blue Heeler and Border Collie dogs into the ute and hitting the track. They have brought a bottle of Moet champagne with them. "A client at my work gave it to me," Leanne says. I don't think they would normally lash out on Moet so it's pretty special and tonight is the night they are going to bring it out. We are definitely not expecting to see them up in the morning by the time we leave. Our little group, on the other hand, is not drinking Moet. We're living it up this evening with a glass of cask wine followed by a cup of hot chocolate.

During the night there is a frantic, excited barking from the dogs and a thundering of feet. A herd of about 20 camels has come charging through the camp, stirring up Leanne and Darryl's dogs and then stampeding away, their big padded feet pounding past back into the bush.

Six Can Camp: Well 49

Nonie and Stuart have been growing sprouts. Yes, all the way along they have had a little garden in the back of their car, carefully watched and watered. Then, "I'm a mother!" Nonie had exclaimed, five days in. She has been, for a long time actually, but this is different. Tiny green leaves had appeared on top of the damp cotton wool. From then on our very basic lunches—tuna on a wrap again?—are topped with a sprinkle of fresh sprouts.

It may be a simple life, but every evening we eat so well. We take turns cooking and have produced some memorable meals. Sometimes we even finish it with chestnuts roasted or marshmallows toasted in the campfire. But by now, apart from those sprouts, and a bag of oranges, there is nothing fresh.

In fact, when we were planning this trip, Nonie and I realised that we would need to provision for 50 days without any chance to shop. So we each dreamed up 25 evening meals, using just tinned and dry ingredients.

Tonight's dinner is a special moment for me—created entirely out of cans. Six cans, in fact: Tiny Taters, cannelloni beans, corn, peas and… the camper's friend, Chilli con carne in a can, Dynamite Stagg. MasterChef eat your heart out, I am now the Queen of Cans.

But no matter what the menu, it does always taste good eating out under the great bowl of stars, with the moon rising over the horizon. We sit by the campfire and watch the Southern Cross sliding slowly across the sky, listening to Pink Floyd's "Dark Side of the Moon" cranked up loud.

We decide to stay two nights. It is another lovely campsite, under those soft and gentle Desert Oaks again, with the soughing of the wind through the branches. And we are so close to the end of the Canning, it is nice to take a moment to absorb it. But we are getting to our destination just in time; the last of the biscuits for morning tea went yesterday, a Monte Carlo. (The Kingstons went a long time ago, of course.)

If you want to strip away the stress of city life, this is a great way to do it. We get up at bird o'clock, when the birds are starting to wake up and there is just the first rim of fiery red along the horizon. And in the evening we eat at fly o'clock, when the flies have left for the night.

The sunrises and sunsets are extravagantly spectacular, throwing waves of scarlet and gold across the sky to start and finish each day. In the daytime hours in between we live a peasant lifestyle, revelling in the simplicity of just spending our day travelling slowly across another short stretch of track, eating when we are hungry and stopping about 3 pm to set up camp for the night.

It is best to be in rhythm with the environment. An early start means the dunes are still damp from the dew, and much easier to cross, and we stop mid-afternoon as they dry out and the sand gets soft and treacherous.

It is like travel at any time in history before the car and the plane introduced the idea of speed. One hundred, two hundred years ago, since time began, this was the only possible pace. Even as the world started to open up, if you set out to visit your relatives in a distant place, by coach or cart, your journey took weeks. Every day was 20, 30 miles and you simply settled back and lived that life for a while until you arrived at your destination.

We don't expect to go fast, and we don't chafe at only covering such a little distance each day. This is the pace that is possible, and we just go with the flow. If we wanted to go fast, we would be on a bitumen road right now, a horrible thought.

Termite Dating Camp: Stretch Lake

Suddenly we are in termite mound country. These intriguing constructions are strangely photogenic pillars of clay, looking like statues. Sometimes they are huge, twice the height of a man, but here in this part of the world, they are little and they look particularly like statues of the Holy Family—now that's kinda weird. But they are out there in their thousands, thickly dotted across the landscape.

Apparently, or so we are told, without termites life as we know it would cease to exist. (I know that you city folk think that without Facebook life as we know it would cease to exist, but let's get even more basic.)

Their story is like a dating site on steroids. The termites live on dead timber. They digest it and convert it into their body protein. Periodically they swarm from the nest in their millions to mate and start new colonies. This is the moment other animals—the lizards, frogs, bats and birds—have been waiting for.

As the cloud of termite hopefuls looking for that special friend hits the open air, it's time to start the party. It is banquet time, a Christmas feast for all those other animals and they don't waste a moment of it. They all get a big protein hit, and that kicks them into making babies too.

In Africa, those huge migrating herds of grass-eating animals thundering across the Serengeti Plain, those David Attenborough favourites, do just the same thing as our little termites. Zebras or wildebeest or elephants turning grass into protein and then becoming breakfast for something else.

Don't you just wish you were up here learning all these fascinating things?

But those termite mounds mean we are in a new part of the country. We have visited the last Well, number 51, and we are about to meet the Tanami Road and head into the Kimberley. Our final camp is beside Stretch Lake which we discover to our surprise has actual water, not salt, and flocks of birds. It is a startling sight after all that red sand. We have emerged from the desert.

The Canning is behind us: 2000 kilometres, 900 sand dunes, some of the most lonely and inhospitable country anywhere in the length and breadth of Australia, with vast spaces, and astounding scenery, and absolute, total silence. If you want to get away from it all, this is a perfect place to try the idea out, it's about as far away as you can get.

In Sydney as we all sat poring over a map, thinking where to go and wondering about the Canning, Nonie had declared emphatically, "No way I'm doing that! Are you kidding, all those corrugations, all those sand dunes, and so remote!"

Yep, that is all absolutely true, the corros, the dunes, and oh, so very remote. But once it got into our heads we couldn't resist it. And here we are, we have done it, we made it. And we loved it.

Not content with that, though, we continued north towards the very top of the continent, the mighty Mitchell Plateau.

PART III

THE MIGHTY MITCHELL PLATEAU

5,000 BURGERS

The fearsome Mitchell Plateau, with a reputation for trashing cars and turning happy camping trips into disasters, in the end turned out to be a pussy-cat. Or perhaps not quite a pussy-cat, maybe more a lion cub.

Fearful of wrecking our camper trailers we had debated leaving them behind and taking to our tents, but eventually we decided to just poke on up the track and see for ourselves how bad it really is.

Phooey, obviously the people who spoke of it in hushed tones hadn't experienced the he-man corrugations and bone crunching washouts of the Canning Stock Route and the Anne Beadell Highway.

The road does bite you in the backside every now and again though. Just as you are lulled into a false sense of security, rattling along on the gravel, there is a sudden patch of seriously rough stuff with corrugations fierce enough to loosen your teeth. Mostly, though, it is a sort-of graded, sort-of smooth-ish track. After what we had just been over, it felt pretty tame.

All roads—the one road, that is—leads first to Drysdale Station. Like most of the properties up here, it is enormous, a million acres, and was for the first hundred years or so of European pioneering settlement, from the 1880s onwards, a cattle station.

We had expected to be pretty much alone on the Mitchell, but to our surprise, Drysdale is humming. At this time of year the grey nomad traffic is building up all across the Top End. All the Geoffs and Kays leave the cold southern states and stream north to the tropics. And Drysdale, like so many cattle stations ekeing out a precarious existence for all of their history until now, with the tyranny of distance and the constant threat of drought, has suddenly come into a bonanza.

There is fuel for sale, a little shop with some basic supplies, a restaurant and a slab-and-corrugated-iron bar. And a sea of tents and camper trailers. The owners, boot and hat country people, bought Drysdale in the 1980s, worked their butts off for 20 years or so as a cattle station, then moved happily into tourism as it started to take off.

It is easy money compared to the hard, hot and often heartbreaking grind of the cattle industry. You just run the slasher over the grass in a paddock, put up a few very basic amenities and keep making it a bit fancier, if you feel like it, as the traffic grows. And fancier isn't very much so, it usually just means the showers are more frequently hot and there are some tables and chairs arranged around a fire pit. We went for a beer under the string of fairy lights near the rustic bar and ended up staying for a hamburger. A $25 hamburger, Aussie style, with beetroot, pineapple, cheese, bacon, egg. And chips of course.

The chef, Chris, comes from soft, sweet Mansfield down south in Victoria, from a valley with green fields and trees that turn pretty colours in the Autumn. He comes up here to the exact opposite to work in this wild landscape for the dry season, goes home when the monsoon starts and everything shuts down.

"That was a good 'burger," we say.

"I should have it down pat," he replies with a grin. "I did 5,000 of them last year."

Chris tells us that these days the owners spend the wet season enjoying life out on their boat up off the northern coast. It sounds like a nice boat: it sleeps 25. And it uses 25,000 litres of fuel during that time, that's more than $60,000 worth. All from making a bit of space for Mr and Mrs Melbourne to put their caravan for a night.

The main attraction of the Mitchell Plateau lies another day's drive north along the Kalumuburu Road: the Mitchell Falls. Travellers who are well-heeled, or too old, or who don't have a suitable vehicle, or who don't like being really, really dusty, fly in to see the falls from above. There is a fleet of tiny helicopters, with pilots so young they should surely still be at school. Walking in one way and taking the chopper out is popular, too, with a bit of circling around the falls and some commentary thrown in.

We opt to walk both ways. First there is a set of smaller waterfalls, and little pools to skirt around, then a rocky path for a few kilometres. When you reach the Mitchell Falls you wade across the top and round to the other side. Then a final clamber across some boulders leads out to a point to look back.

Suddenly a magical panorama opens out. There are four huge drops, with a great mass of water tumbling down. There is a big, green pool at the bottom of each long splash of white water, before it rushes over the next ledge. It is spectacular, this enormous waterfall surrounded by cliffs of rusty-red rock.

I can't decide if I like the waterfall or the rocks best, actually. The falls are sensational of course, calendar-photo stuff, and rightly famous as the premier tourist attraction of the whole plateau.

But no-one mentions those heart-stoppingly beautiful rocks, loops and whorls of burnished stone, weathered by wind and water over eons, with sensual dips and curves and hollows, and so very smooth that you could easily imagine that they had been sanded smooth and painted with ochre-orange paving paint. The others are already happily swimming in the pool far below, but I am still stuck way back swooning over those rocks. If I were a sculptor, that is what I would like to create.

Gwion Gwion

If you stay at the Mitchell Falls campground, off the road leading north to Kalumuburu, at this time of year you will definitely meet Neil. He is the campground manager, a volunteer from down south, happy to put in a few hours of work a day, pottering around and taking care of things in return for free camping for the season. We pull in. In an instant he has arrived at our side and settled in for a chat.

"No concessions for us oldies," he says to Ren, then looks at me, "and your daughter can't get one either." He laughs happily at his joke.

He is good value. I wonder if the Department of Parks and Water Resources knows just how good. He runs the place, keeps it clean, keeps everyone happy, buzzes around in his little cart, tells you where to swim, where to camp.

He says the toilets over the back are new. "I wonder who designed them, though," he says. "Nice disabled toilets, with wide doors, handrails, room to turn a wheelchair around inside. And… six steps leading up to them." He gives a great hoot of laughter and goes off to tell the story to the next arrival.

That night there is a dingo choir again, that eerie, mournful chorus. There are some children nearby copying them and shrieking with laughter. There must be a lot of dingoes around. "Dingoes have a keen fashion sense," the warning sign reads. "They love to eat the latest in hats and footwear."

The Mitchell Plateau is famous for its Indigenous Gwion Gwion rock art (also called Bradshaw art after the explorer who discovered it in 1891). There seems to be an awful lot of it. Every now and again there is a sign: "Cultural Art Sites." It is always worth stopping for a look. Usually there is a jumble of huge rocks, with lots of flat faces just perfect for a spot of painting some time in prehistory. Where there is an overhang the paintings are still a vibrant red or black.

They are painted in two distinct styles. Some paintings are of heads, rounded, with big eyes and head-dresses like helmets. Erik Von Daniken would go nuts over these; they do look like aliens.

Others could have been copied straight from warriors in New Guinea dressed up for a ceremony; the long, stringy, swaying figures are wearing armbands, tassels and pointed headgear.

Of course, New Guinea isn't very far away. It is just 2,000 kilometres north-east of here (and it is only 500 kilometres directly north of Cape York). The land bridge between the two countries was still there until just 6,000 years ago, and as it gradually went underwater people drifted south. That would explain the similarities. Until recently the local Aboriginal people used to dress up like these painted warriors for their corroborees. And apparently in East Arnhem land, directly east of here, they still do.

We walk around these rocks covered in the fantastic paintings, staring at it all, discovering another and yet another rock face crammed with artwork. Who did these, and what do they mean? We are dazzled by the sheer number of pictures and love that we can simply wander around finding them and walk (and often climb) right up close to them. No barriers, no tickets, no crowds. Sometimes there is a bit of fence, just to stop cattle from rubbing against them.

In the middle of one set of rocks is something that stops us in our tracks: three skulls and some leg bones on a ledge. Just tucked in there, for who would know how many thousands of years. We stare at them, then Stuart suddenly says, "That one on the left didn't have a very happy ending. He has a big hole in his forehead." We look again. There is indeed an ugly-looking chunk out of the bone. We spend a long time just standing looking, taking all of that in.

Honeymoon Bay

We are heading for the coast, further and further north. Of course, it is getting hotter as we go, and there will be the big blue ocean when we get there. But this is now crocodile country, so there will be no swimming. Nonie has developed a croc phobia. "100% chance of being eaten," she repeats regularly in a horrified tone of voice, quoting from a book she has read.

It doesn't sound like something I would like to test out. The last time we had access to the news, a couple of weeks and thousands of kilometres ago, we read that a woman, wading in knee-deep water with a friend, had been taken by a croc in Queensland.

That daunting information was followed rapidly by news of another attack on two old guys fishing in a little tinny in the Northern Territory. Not a good way to go, grabbed in a split-second by those mighty jaws and rolled underwater to drown, then stashed in a submerged tree to snack on at leisure.

But we do want to drive as far as we can up here, just for the satisfaction of going as far as we can and having a look. There is a fishing spot we have heard of that sounds spectacular, so we go to check it out. If it is as beautiful as it looks in the book on the region we might stay there for a few days. When we arrive, it does seem pretty ramshackle, but that's not unusual out here.

There are a couple of Outback characters sitting in the shade of a rusty veranda roof. The long, thin one with the antique thongs and the hacking smoker's cough seems to be in charge. His mate, a big brown-skinned man filling a camp chair, is nursing a rifle with a telescopic sight. Someone has made a determined attempt to bash in the two windows next to him. They say hello in a guarded sort of way and stare steadily at us. It is just a little bit too Deliverance, so we get a fill of fuel from the tanker on the jetty and go on our way.

The other place to try, Honeymoon Bay, was recommended to us by the dirt bike boys we met on the Canning Stock Route. "You can get oysters off the rocks there," they had said enthusiastically.

You are not permitted to take more fish or oysters than you can eat on the same day. But—hang on a minute—if we are to prise them off the rocks and eat them then and there doesn't that mean that we will be right down at the edge of the ocean? Where the crocs are? Do the crocs also abide by the rule only to take as much as they can eat in one day? And if so, which one of us will it be?

Not Nonie, that's for sure. She isn't going anywhere near that water. She might not even get out of the car. She is completely freaked out by everything she has read about how to Be CrocWise! so of course Sod's Law comes into operation and they get bogged in deep sand right near the waters' edge.

Everyone gets out to have a look and work out what to do. Except Nonie, she is sitting rigidly in the car. Even the windows are wound up, as if a croc could shoot out of the water and dive head-first into the passenger seat.

When something happens in the Outback, anyone that is around will drift in to look, make suggestions, and help. Any mechanical—or in this case, bogging—event is a bloke magnet, and sure enough some friendly nearby campers cheerfully get their winch into action.

Ren goes over with two shovels, one for him and an extra one for Nonie to dig sand out from under the wheels. That is definitely not going to happen. She stays firmly in her vehicle. But eventually their car gets out. Everyone survives.

Our new helpful friends have been coming here for years and explain how they go swimming.

"We put the boat in the water between us and the crocs and one of us goes in with the kiddies and one watches from the shore." Very relaxing.

The only town on the Mitchell Plateau is Kalumburu, a small Aboriginal community right at the top. It has been a Catholic mission run by the Benedictine order for 50 years. When we get there a young man wanders up and looks in the window of our car, offering paintings at

$25 a pop. He has a couple of copies of the Bradshaw art we have seen rolled up in his hand.

"Everythin' shut today, bit of stealin' trouble," he says. Apparently there was a robbery at the shop last night and everything is shut tight. I look at this bloke, young, fit, good-looking, and wonder about his life. We have thought about this a lot; there doesn't seem to be any work except painting Indigenous art or possibly as a ranger. What do people do here? What can they do? And if they leave, where would they go?

In so many Outback places the First Nations people still speak their native language every day. Aboriginal languages, of which there are hundreds, have huge vocabularies—far more words than English—and are rich with myth and poetry. But their English is rudimentary, grammatically mixed and heavily accented. It is almost a dialect of English, but not one that would enable them to get anything but the lowest level of work in a city or even a country town.

There is a lot of emphasis on trying to raise school attendance in Indigenous communities, but if a child does go through school, where could that lead, in a place as remote as this? We wonder about it, but we have no idea what the answer might be.

Kalumburu is intriguing. Most Aboriginal communities are desolate dust-bowls. Depressing and forlorn, with broken-down cars abandoned around the edges and miserable mangy dogs everywhere. Here, something seems to be different. The houses are trim, with fences and bits of garden. A man is watering a lawn. Down a side street a couple of blokes in work clothes are picking up rubbish.

A little boy comes out of a gate with his grandfather. His hair has never been combed and he has bare feet, but he is wearing a school uniform t-shirt and clutching a school lunch and a popper of juice.

I stop to take a photo of a mural on the shop wall. "Good morning," says a woman sitting in a car beside me, with a friendly smile. On the shop are signs: "No School: No Shop" for the kids. And for the adults: "No Drugs", "No Alcohol".

This top half of the Mitchell Plateau suddenly looks very tropical. It reminds us of Cape York—not surprising as it is about the same latitude. It is a long way north of Cairns, even a long way north of Cooktown.

It is the sort of scenery that would suit a movie. Pandanus palms make their appearance. The creeks have a bit of water with some tumbled stones and clusters of plants around the edge. A massive snake, at least two metres long and as thick as your wrist, is lying across the road. It rears up, swerves away and vanishes into the long grass.

The landscape to the horizon is changing too. Instead of the flat, red spinifex-covered vistas we have been used to for the last few weeks there are now rolling hills, covered with spindly green trees.

The road winds, curves and swoops up the hills and down to the creek crossings. It is a road best treated with respect. There is a scattering of parts from vehicles all along the way: body panels, an air intake for a snorkel, an engine mounting. If you are careless it exacts a nasty price.

Ren has just taken a photo of a particularly vicious rocky patch when around the next corner there is a government sign proudly announcing "Roads to Recovery." We are still laughing when the next lot of corrugations start.

We have gone as far north as we can. We can almost see Indonesia from here, just 2,000 kilometres away. And Timor is a just hop at 600 kilometres, over a little bit of ocean. So we turn south and head back towards the Gibb River Road. Weirdly, it seems a lot closer to home than it used to. Everything is relative, I guess.

PART IV

THE HAY RIVER TRACK

BACK TO BIRDSVILLE

It is nice to get home, to catch up with friends and family, to get back to a life of eating out, watching television and enjoying long, hot showers. But it only takes a few months in the city to get itchy feet again. Where to go next? Let's head for Birdsville.

The last time we came to Birdsville, three years ago, we had a big surprise. We had crawled across the Simpson Desert, a desolate stretch of 1000 sand dunes spread west to east in the very middle of Australia, and were ready to roll into tiny, remote Birdsville, just a flyspeck on the map, and wrap ourselves around a long, cold beer.

A name like Birdsville is a bit of a giveaway: don't get your hopes up. There's not much there, just a straggle of low buildings on a dusty road, and a very old pub. It is right in the middle of the country, and it is a very big country.

To get to the centre of Australia from any direction is a long, long way. If it was Europe, just to get there you would cross several international borders, and change languages half a dozen times. If it was the USA there would be strings of cowboy and gingham towns and cities along the way. But in Australia it is mostly just long stretches of nothing, with nothing there at the end. So of course, Birdsville is a sleepy little town most of the year.

But on that occasion, after a week of total isolation along the Simpson Desert track, we had clambered over Big Red, the last and biggest sand dune of the whole 1000 and to our utter astonishment found ourselves looking down on a bustling hive of activity. The place was full of huge trucks, tents and Port-a-loos. What?

As we came down, wide-eyed and perplexed, we discovered that it was the remains of a huge, three-day outdoor concert with Big Red as the backdrop. Jimmy Barnes, the Aussie rock legend, had been headlining. They were bumping out the stage. The last of the revellers were straggling away.

We stared in amazement. Who would come all this way for that? Thousands, that's who, from the opposite direction, up the Birdsville Track, to rave in the Outback. Every camping spot in the town was packed and the pub ran out of food.

So, now we are heading back to do another cast at the Simpson, this time starting at the Birdsville end, and to our astonishment what do we see happening? Four-wheel-drive vehicles converging from everywhere. There are tell-tale puffs of dust strung out in lines to the horizon as vehicles converge on Birdsville. Someone tells us that the view from the air is like a scene from Mad Max.

Incredibly, it is that concert again, with Australia's iconic singers lining up (will Johnny Farnham ever stop?) and this time, twice as many ravers. Birdsville is heaving with beanies and tattoos. The music is pumping already and there are crowds outside the little bakery waiting for the camel pies to come out of the oven. The Big Red Bash.

North of Big Red

But Birdsville is just a waypoint for us. This time, we are heading north. If you look at a map, you can make out a little dotted line, 150 kilometres west of Birdsville, just above Poeppel Corner. (Augustus Poeppel was the surveyor who worked in this area in the late 1880s, creating as part of his job a special place where you can stand with your two boots in three states at once: Queensland, Northern Territory and South Australia. The most popular photographic scene at Poeppel corner? Feet.)

There is a lot of traffic coming across the Simpson from the west. That adventure trail is becoming more and more popular, starting at the hot Dalhousie Springs and ending 400 kilometres later with the final blokey flourish of an engine-screaming, tyre-spinning attempt to cross Big Red at its highest, softest part.

Of course, a lot of traffic is a relative number, but it is enough so that, even with a sand flag waving high above the vehicle to warn of your approach, everyone is calling ahead on Channel 10 on the two-way radio.

"Two vehicles travelling east, 12 kilometres from Big Red."

"Copy that, party of two on this side, we'll wait for you to come over."

"Got a visual on you now."

No-one wants to meet another vehicle head-on at the top of a sand dune, no matter how slowly you are going.

Those cars are all heading for Birdsville, but we are just passing through to meet the start of the Hay River Track, at the eastern edge of the Simpson. We don't expect to meet any other travellers between here and Jervois Station, a week or so away. Because this track runs south to north, much of it lies in the flat sweeps of land between the sand dunes—the swales—and the going should be easier.

But to get to the place where the track turns north, we first have to cross 124 sand dunes. These are always lots of fun: a bit of a roller-coaster ride, or a long steep slope of red dirt, with no way of knowing if it will be an easy pull up and over the top or if there will be surprising patches of bumps and hollows on the other side. Sometimes the track turns sharply at the very top of a crest, sometimes there is an unexpected patch of loose, soft sand.

Of course, sometimes you just don't quite make it. The vehicle struggles gamely up, slower and slower, and then comes to a halt lodged in soft sand, often tantalisingly close to the crest. Back down, try again, give it a bit more, or go a bit slower. Let a bit more air out of the tyres. Get a better run-up. Get out the snatch strap or start up the winch. It's all part of the fun, and part of getting where we want to go.

Usually where we want to go means somewhere we haven't been before. And we haven't crossed the Simpson on the Hay River Track. It will be a hard, dry drive.

Of course, the First Nations people have lived all over this area for countless thousands of years, at least 60,000. They survived perfectly well in this incredibly harsh and unforgiving environment, moving in small hunter-gatherer groups. It is hard to imagine. Sparse patches of sun-baked vegetation and gnarled and wind-twisted trees are dotted across the swales, interspersed here and there with little clumps of wispy native grasses. It looks far too arid to support life.

There is spinifex, of course, that deceptive plant that looks so soft, but has needle-sharp filaments. Each tussock is a little world of insects and tiny animals. They leave sets of miniature footprints in the sand. There were enough seeds and little lizards and tiny mammals to

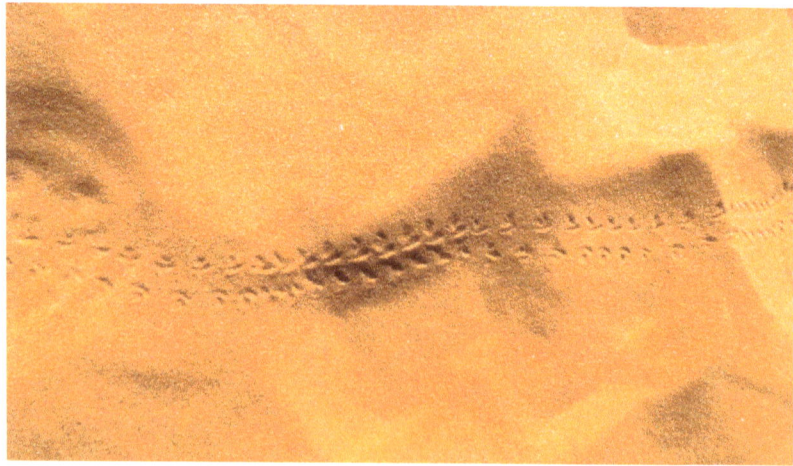

support family groups and the Aboriginal people tended native wells to get just sufficient water to stay alive.

Then during the late 1800s the Europeans started exploring. The maps are criss-crossed with the traces of their heroic attempts to explore and map these mysterious regions and to try to find the elusive "Inland Sea" that by all European logic must be out there somewhere.

The Gibson Desert is named after one unlucky explorer who was sent to get help for his party and was never seen again. Landforms are named after other explorers who battled through. (And named after the experiences they were having. Mount Disappointment seems to figure fairly regularly across Australia.)

One of the most successful expeditions was led by Dr C T Madigan, who undertook a well-equipped scientific venture in 1939 with nine men and nineteen camels, crossing the Simpson from west to east. Hmm, that Madigan Line looks really interesting, it is apparently a very difficult track. We pore over the map and do calculations of fuel and water for future adventures.

Our little red track develops into a soft ride, sandy and narrow, weaving its way along the swales, with a dune every now and again. It does wander rather a lot, turning and twisting. Maybe the grader driver hit the turps a bit too much and had trouble seeing in a straight line next morning.

Each day we make a little progress, at about 20 kilometres an hour, and end it with a campfire and a ringside view of the stars. The air, dry and crisp, feels as if it has just been washed clean. The days are cool, and the nights are freezing, down to -4 degrees. (Wearing a beanie in bed is a particularly fetching look.) We sit by the campfire, chatting, with a glass of red, then turn in early ready for the next day.

Halfway along, we take a detour to Lake Caroline. Don't be misled, these lakes and rivers are blue on the GPS, but there's no blue in them. And, on the very rare occasions when they are blue, you don't want to be anywhere near them, as the floodwaters sweep across the area, spilling over the banks and turning huge expanses of flat country, just for a few weeks, into that inland sea. Then they drain, and it might not rain again for years.

But Lake Caroline sounds nice, so we go to have a look. A couple of people had told us that they turned back from that track because it was too sandy. But we decide to have a go anyway. Nonie and Stu go through the first soft bit, no problem, but we grind to a halt, our wheels axle-deep in sand. We let down the tyres a bit more, but it is still too soft underfoot. "Oh goody," says Stuart, visibly excited to have the chance to play with the winch.

We hook it onto a tree, but the line is too short to pull us out. So, using the other vehicle up ahead, with the winch and a snatch strap all in play, we inch forward and gradually get our tyres onto firm ground.

It is certainly a lovely drive out to the lake, a rolling vista of sandhill and scrub, nicely dotted and varied, with small, tastefully placed outcrops of orange rock to make a lovely panorama.

When we reach the lake, it is an expanse of dried mud, cracked into geometric shapes and spread out flat to the horizon. It is not the sort of place you want to find yourself in with even a drop of rain, if you plan to get out again ahead of next month.

We fool around a bit, lying on the dried clay (as you do), taking group selfies, and looking at the tracks of camels, pressed into the mud and leading off into the distance. But it is not the place to camp, so back the 11 kilometres to the track, over that super-soft patch without any trouble this time.

There has been no letup from the bitterly cold Westerly wind that has been blowing day and night but surely, we think, as we cross the Tropic of Capricorn, it must get warmer soon.

If you are a thirsty dingo, what would you do? Visit a dingo well, of course. We find one beside the track, complete with a nice explanation. When the aborigines left the area, as the Europeans pushed them into missions, the native wells that they had carefully tended vanished along with them.

So the dingoes, the apex predators, died out too. This messed up the whole natural ecology of the area. Some bright spark in a government department somewhere decided to put in a bore, and a trough. Smart move—the dingo population has steadily increased and everything is improving. We fill our tank from the tap thoughtfully provided for travellers, and make camp more than one kilometre away, as requested on the sign.

We have heard about Batton Hill Camp, an Aboriginal Native Title property, now returned to the traditional owners, the Atnetye people. It sounds like a good place to stay, with basic facilities for visitors. Plenty of water, for example, for that rare luxury—long, hot showers heated by a donkey engine. After washing for days in an inch of water, the idea is really tempting, and we are all ready for a rest day.

We have been on the road now for two weeks, and with no internet or phone for the last six days. We have no idea what has happened in the world. And blissfully wandering along those sandy tracks, we just don't care.

Boulia or Bust

The first time we came to Boulia, in 1975, we had no satellite phone (of course) and no mobile phone (of course). We were on a six-week trip to Ayers Rock (as it was then called) and beyond. We were young and fearless (and with a three-month-old baby).

By the time we got back to Sydney we had fallen in love, permanently and passionately, with the fierce landscapes of the Outback. And Boulia was one of those sleepy little dots on the map that we remembered.

The next time, six years ago, we were still the only car in the street. Boulia, as usual, was dozing in the midday sun. But now, as we drive in, it looks very different. Between the last stragglers from the Big Red Bash going home and the Grey Nomads heading north for the winter, the place is buzzing with caravans and campers.

The little shop has a note in the window hopefully advertising for casual staff and there is a queue at the service station waiting for fuel. The word on the street is that there has been a 500% increase in tourism, and we can see it.

But although we like neat'n'tidy little Boulia we are here for another reason. We have popped out of the northern end of the Hay River Track and turned east along the Plenty Highway. This is another one of those "highways" that are punishingly rough, but we are there for a purpose. Nonie has a friend who grew up on a property 30 kilometres out of town, and we have been invited to visit her nephew and his wife and children.

We roll in, late in the day, hot and dusty, down the three-kilometre front drive to the homestead, to make the acquaintance of the family.

If you made a movie of the Outback and you wanted to cast the perfect character in it, you would want to find Brook McGlinchey, the owner of Bedalia Station. Tall and rangy, with a big hat and a slow manner, he strolls over to say (what else but) "G'day." He has the steady stare of a man used to checking out cattle in a distant paddock.

After a while he squats on his haunches, snapping bit of stick while he talks. One of his children, in a big hat matching his father's, is playing with a toy truck in the dirt. Another small boy is climbing a tree. Brook's wife Sarah, slight, blonde and laid-back, comes out of the house with a little girl.

We all stand chatting, while the boys ride around on their PeeWee 50cc motorbikes. They dart off to ride the fenceline around the big house paddock, disappearing out of sight. No-one turns a hair. They are four and six years old. Sarah is a full-time mother, of course. Out here that's just the way it is. She has her kids, and her horses. She used to ride as a jockey in camel races and came second one time in camel racing's Melbourne Cup.

Her lifestyle certainly seems to suit her. She looks very relaxed and has plenty of time to chat. Like so many bush mothers, she teaches her oldest child, Sam, with the aid of the School of the Air. She will do that for all of them until they reach High School. Then what? "Boarding school is so expensive," she says. "And Brook really only went there for the sport, so that was a bit of a waste. We'll just wait and see."

After dark they come over to visit. The kids are in their pyjamas, running around the campfire and investigating our camper trailers. There is a small grave nearby with a headstone: RIP My Good Mate Memphis. "He was a real good dog," says Brook slowly. "We lose a lot of 'em to brown snakes."

It's a great lifestyle, but can you make a living from a place like this? Apparently yes. The McGlincheys have been in the area for 100 years, and on this farm for more than 50. Brook's mother Nina still lives in the big homestead, and Brook hopes one of his children will take over after him.

"But another 200 would be good, much more profit with not much more costs." Another two hundred? Two hundred thousand, that is. Acres. It is huge numbers out here. There is not much rainfall but it doesn't need much, a little bit makes a big difference. "It's sweet re-sponding land," Brook says fondly, looking out at it with his thousand-yard stare.

Dinosaur Country

Abound 95 million years ago, as the tectonic plates moved around, the gigantic southern land mass of Gondwanaland made a slow slide northward, gradually separating into Australia, South America and Antarctica. In this part of the world the climate was moist and the vegetation was lush. And around Winton those were delightful conditions for dinosaurs, apparently, because there were a lot of them across this whole region.

One incredible place, Lark Quarry, has the distinction of being the only place on earth where you can see the evidence of a dinosaur stampede. How could we resist that? We are on our way to have a look, travelling east into the middle of Queensland.

In the 1960s a local found some stones with what looked like bird footprints. He took them to the pub and someone thought they looked interesting. By pure chance there happened to be an expert having a drink there that day and he said, "What you've got is dinosaur footprints."

"Yeah, mate, pull the other one."

But, amazingly, they were indeed dinosaur footprints and only discovered by a series of lucky chances: the original stampede event being covered by a layer of sand then a thin layer of ironstone; the curiosity of a local farmer; and the highly unlikely chance that a scientist happened to be at the pub when he brought the stones in to show his mates.

What was revealed was over 3,000 footprints of three different types of dinosaur in one spot next to a prehistoric lake. It looks as if one big dinosaur came stomping in (there they are, huge clawed footprints in the stone, striding in) followed by hundreds of small dinosaurs rushing away in panic. The marks left in the mud are so clear, so striking, it is easy to imagine the scene laid out right there. To stand just a metre above the actual place it happened is riveting.

But then, having stared and exclaimed, it is time to look for somewhere to camp. We find the perfect spot on the edge of a rocky ravine, with stunning views across to the red rock hills in the distance, and after watching the blood-red sun drop below the horizon, to eat dinner and then settle down to watch a movie on the laptop under the stars.

BANJO MANIA

Winton is famous for its dinosaurs, but it has another claim to fame, close to Australia's heart. One of our heroes is bush poet Banjo Paterson. Remember Flash Jack from Gundagai? Banjo Paterson included that in a collection of poetry in 1905. And he also wrote our de facto national anthem, Waltzing Matilda. He first performed it in a pub here in Winton in 1895. It was an instant hit and swept the country.

Other countries have their songs of courage and derring-do: soldiers and cowboys. Our favourite song tells the story of a swaggie who steals a sheep and, rather than be caught by the police, jumps into a waterhole to drown. Stirring, heroic sentiments! Never mind, it is part of the national psyche anyway, and it has stayed popular ever since.

In fact, when we gave up singing God Save Our Gracious Queen as a national anthem, it almost got voted in as the replacement. And Winton just loves it. Everything is Banjo this or Waltzing Matilda that.

We walk past the Banjo Bistro and the information centre is the Waltzing Matilda Centre. Everything new and tourist-oriented is designed with artistic slabs of rusty metal and corrugated iron with something Banjo attached, and there is a hint of haybales and old leather around every corner.

So with all that memorabilia on every side, we are more than surprised to find a Council art gallery packed with astounding modern paintings. Name a famous Australian artist (hint: Sidney Nolan, John Olsen, Margaret Olley, Arthur Boyd… I could go on and on) and they are in there. One painting for each artist, and every one a peach. We walk around staring at them, exclaiming in amazement, then do the rounds again, and then one more time before we tear ourselves away.

Just to bring us back to earth again, we find another artistic triumph just down the road—Arno's Wall. The local junkyard has been transformed by a high wall around the premises with items from the collection embedded into the concrete. An old motorbike? Whack it in the wall, mate. A pump, a sewing machine, some piping? In the wall. What about all these hubcaps? Make 'em into a gate. And along the top of the wall, lots of little pointy bits of rusty junk, like crenellations on some mad castle. Fabulous.

Revenge

What would be a good way to get sweet revenge on a wife you really, really didn't like? You could do it Mr MacDonald's way.

Sweet little Croydon in western Queensland, now home to less than 400 people, was a goldmining hub in the late 1800s. By late 1886 the new town's population had passed 6500 and there were, according to legend, something like 90 hotels on the diggings.

These days it boasts a particularly well-preserved historic precinct. Full of the usual old relics and photos, but with the buildings all nicely painted and in good repair. There is the old Courthouse, complete with carboard cut-outs for the bewhiskered judge, the drooping prisoner and the stolid police officer. There is the goldrush-era Police Station, with antique handcuffs and revolvers. And, of course, there is the stately Victorian-style Town Hall, with the predictable photos of past mayors and local identities.

But what's this about the hospital, built in 1894 and so unusually large and well-equipped for its day? Apparently local identity Mr MacDonald, who had very deep pockets, left a massive sum to the hospital in his will—forty thousand pounds, an absolute fortune. And to his wife? He left her "one shilling, to buy a rope to hang herself." Right.

Cobbold Gorge

After being surprised by Croydon, we are heading for Cobbold Gorge, which is a well-known tourist attraction. There is a brochure in every town along the way, with nice-looking pictures of rocky stuff. That's not unexpected. We are out of the desert and climbing into the Great Dividing Range again, so there will be cliffs and rocks. But we decide to check it out anyway.

In 1867, a young boy, Frank Cobbold, set out for Australia, hoping for adventure. He was only 14 when he left, but he sailed alone, and in a long story of lots of vision and even more hard work, ended up owning a whole swag of huge cattle properties across Queensland. Another of those rags-to-riches stories.

At the very same time, Paddy Durack was also pioneering in South-Western Queensland and the Kimberley, and Stanley Kidman was creating his string of cattle stations from North to South across the whole country. A map showing all of the properties of these three men would be like a jig-saw puzzle of at least half of the continent.

Frank Cobbold did not have any children to inherit his properties, but he and his wife left his huge fortune to various charities in the region. Although he did not actually own this particular property, he certainly visited it, and was regarded with great respect throughout the whole area.

So the magnificent gorge is named after him and his story is everywhere here, with photos of him on horseback, with dogs and cattle beside a river, and in his dress suit, his hair neatly brushed and his beard trimmed, looking serious and prosperous.

The present owners of this property, Simon Terry and his four brothers and two sisters, did inherit it from their parents and are busy transforming it. It is still a working cattle station with 12,000 Brahman cattle, but the tourist attraction side of it is growing and growing.

As a schoolboy in the 1990s Simon used to take friends to see something spectacular that he had discovered deep the station: a gorge, long, deep and very, very narrow, snaking along with a still green river at the bottom.

The gorge is young, only about 10,000 years old. It was probably formed when there was a sudden split in the land, and the soft sandstone was then sculpted by successive floods into high curving walls.

We pile into a flat-bottomed boat and glide silently along. It is so narrow that the boat can barely fit. Sometimes it scrapes gently through. The sky is a sliver of blue high above. The rock walls swoop in and out. It has that cathedral feeling, and the chattering group falls silent as we all gaze up in awe.

It is a natural wonder that attracts thousands of people every year. From that simple beginning, as the word got out more and more people wanted to come and have a look. This year they expect about 17,000 visitors.

It is all family-run, plus a staff of cheerful European backpackers and some country-style guides. And it is nicely done, Outback style with some camping, some cabins and a bush-timber restaurant. You can also take the heavily promoted helicopter tour to see it all from the air or (this is a surprise) you can have a cocktail by the infinity-edge swimming pool. Time for a dip.

PART V

CAPE YORK

ROADSIDE REPAIRS

A week ago we were climbing over sand dunes, covered in red dust and gazing at far horizons. Now we are surrounded by the close, lush green of a sub-tropical rain forest. We have left the Hay River Track far behind us and are and headed for North Queensland.

"Beautiful One Day, Perfect the Next," declares the tourist advertising, aimed at people from the south. Those Queenslanders feel pretty superior. "Why would you choose to live down there," they reason, "where it is cold and crowded and everyone rushes around all the time?" Maybe they have a point, and we are on our way to check it out.

First stop Atherton. Not by choice. A week ago, Ren gave the bearings on our camper trailer a little test feel, as he does, and they were worryingly hot. Not a good sign. So Roadside Repairs had swung into action.

Mechanical things are definitely men's work out here, Stu and Ren taking greasy things apart and staring at them. It wasn't long before another car stopped and a bloke strolled over, hands in his pockets. He just nodded and hunkered down to look.

Before long there were three heads bent over the wheel, deep in thought. Over the next half-hour our new friend trotted back and forth to his vehicle, fetching useful bits and pieces. Note to self: if you need a tool you don't have, find a retired engineer.

They put it back together with some banging noises and all went well. But we needed to arrange a proper fix, so it was off to Atherton, the nearest town with a mechanic. And we waited. For a day… two days…the part arrived, but it was the wrong part…the days stretched into a week. So what do you do in Atherton to fill in time?

Although it is a long way north, it is high, hilly country a with lots of waterfalls, and little rocky streams that roar with water in the wet season. So the climate is relatively cool. The farms are green, and the cattle are sleek and fat. It is quite a culture shock after the desert to be looking at all that vivid green grass and to stop at roadside attractions selling artisan cheese.

We tick off everything to do in the area. Take the walk beside the creek to find a platypus, a turtle, a tree kangaroo. Take photographs of the waterfalls. Comment on how pretty it all is. Take photographs of trees. But that sweet, green landscape is a bit too soft for us, so when the mechanic finally finishes the job we are off like a shot.

We are pointed towards Cape York, the very northernmost tip of Australia.

First stop the Daintree National Park. It is still very lush, but wilder.

The rolling hills are much steeper, topped with mist and covered with thick rainforest. The kind of country, they say, where you could plant a nail and grow a crowbar. There are palms and ferns. And there is the Daintree River, invitingly cool. Don't be fooled, though—it is full of crocodiles.

In Australia it is good to know the difference between freshwater and saltwater crocs. Freshies will give you a nip if you really annoy them. (Just wondering—how bored would you have to be to amuse yourself by annoying a crocodile?)

But here's where it gets really serious, salties will pursue you and eat you, sliding silently through the water and then grabbing you with a snap of their terrifying jaws. They perfected their hunting technique in the age of the dinosaurs and have had no need to change it since.

There are Achtung!! signs everywhere an unwary tourist might fall for the spell of the exquisite blue water of these tropical beaches or the cool allure of the rivers. Still, every year someone decides to chance their luck and becomes another statistic. Not a good way to go.

We settle for a dawn boat trip to look for birds. We see 29 varieties right here plus a couple of early morning crocs out for a bit of breakfast. The birds are really lovely, it is a birdwatcher's paradise. But the crocs are chilling, the armour-plated tails lazily propelling them through the water, their eyes glittering just above the surface.

The Crazy CREB Track

If your idea of fun is climbing up steep, rough clay hills, with massive ruts and a good chance of slipping and sliding, the CREB track might be just your thing.

Years ago, the Carpentaria Regional Electricity Board decided to put power lines across the Daintree wilderness. So they did. Straight across, from A to B. And the road to service them? Straight across that steep mountainous country. Some engineer somewhere drew a line along the map with a ruler. No pandering to the faint-hearted by going around any hills, it was just up and over, straight ahead Fred.

We had been across it before and it had been, well, memorable.

So, it is irresistible to have another go at it. This time it will give our friends a thrill too. Now we are six. Arthur and Merren have joined the happy gang, with a newish camper trailer. Arthur is keen to learn about 4-wheel driving. Merren is keen to learn about how to be more excited than terrified. So far both are progressing well and the CREB track will certainly give them a masterclass.

It is just a slice through the bush, through truly beautiful country. The steep hills are covered with mighty trees and velvety green undergrowth. Of course, when you are fully engaged in rocking up and over crests and hollows, trying to stay on the road to avoid sliding over the edge and crashing down the mountainside, the scenery is a bit of a blur.

Even a drop of rain makes this track impassable, and there had been a little bit a few days ago, so the clay is still sticky, tacky, slippery. We race up, drop sideways into ruts, stagger to the top of the hill then clamber over to see what the other side brings.

I'm too busy hanging on and looking out for big holes to properly take in Merren's face, but when I do catch a glimpse it is the kind of wide-eyed terror that you might see at the top of a roller-coaster. She's not screaming, though, or demanding to get out and walk, so she's doing well for a beginner.

We spend the day on the CREB, and it is just as much fun as before. The kind of fun that you really like to look back on, having made it out the other end.

But, enough of playtime, we have work to do. We are heading steadily north, and there is a long way to go before we reach The Tip.

THE DARWIN AWARD

There's brave and there's stupid. Up here in the north of Australia you get a lot of both.

The brave ones end up in photographs on the walls of roadhouses, standing in shorts, boots and hat (and nothing else, forget the socks or shirts), usually beside an enormous wheel or an enormous fish.

Toots, the Legend of the Cape, is especially famous up here. She was a truck driver and a chick, that picked her out of the crowd for starters. But Toots was much more. She was always the first truck through after The Wet, the six months of monsoonal rain that floods all the rivers, closes the roads and shuts down the little car ferries.

There is so much rain in The Wet that they measure the rivers up here in SydHarbs—the number of volumes of Sydney Harbour that flow down in a day. Then as The Dry begins the roads start to open, with the tracks just waiting to bog vehicles, and some of the rivers still up to the truck doors.

Toots would load up then and struggle gamely through with a truck full of the essentials for the stranded locals, stomping around in the mud with her big boots and her big smile. She was tragically killed when a crane swung the wrong way and crushed her against her truck just as she was about to set out again, at age 58. There is a monument to her, and a song.

And then there were Dick Mathews and Hector Macquarrie, who drove a Baby Austin, with all of 7 horsepower, to The Tip in 1928. Floating her across rivers on a makeshift barge, pulling her out of sand with horses, but battling dauntlessly on. And let's not forget the explorers: starved, sick, and speared. There is a striking painting of Edmund Kennedy in 1848, dying exactly that way.

Then there is stupid, the blokes who are up for a Darwin Award. Charles Darwin, that is. They stand knee-deep in rivers just next to the crocodile warning signs, or fish from the bank within easy lunging range. They crash twice too fast along rutted tracks, destroying their tail shafts and axles. Or they race through creeks without knowing if there is a big rock or a nasty hole under the water. Hello hole…goodbye car…hello crocodile.

These days, this part of Cape York is a mix of farming and tourism. But to begin with, mostly it was about gold. In the 1880s, as one find after another was made, canvas towns erupted like mushrooms, and disappeared just as fast. Prospectors made fortunes, and blew them at the slab hut pubs, handing their money over the counter to the barman and drinking until it was gone. There were pubs like that everywhere.

We pull in at one of them, the Lion's Den Hotel, where hopeful prospectors stopped before they trooped off into the wild. There is a good collection of rusty old artefacts, the usual photograph of a gaggle of kids lined up in front of an old schoolroom in about 1890, and a bar that has not been renovated since then.

We buy a beer and settle down under the shady veranda to listen to a singer. He is accompanied by a washboard player and a tea-chest base, and they are putting out some lazy blues. All the old favourites one after the other. And there is, of course, one he wrote to an old mate who died. The performer almost certainly drifted in here 20 years ago, had a beer, played a few bars, and just stayed on.

People stroll in, sit for a while, then wander off, heading north into Cape York. It really is a tradie paradise up here. They are all Jared, Darren or Aaron. They all wear shorts, thongs and a baseball cap. They all drive vehicles bought tax-deductible through their plumbing or tiling businesses, because of course you need a fully kitted out 4X4 for work, including the winch, the swag and the two-way radio.

They talk cars and football. They cheer when their mates make it through a creek crossing. They say g'day, with a nod. They are always in a good mood, having the time of their life. They are young and fit and easy-going. If I needed them to push my car, or lift a heavy weight, they would be there in a flash, then disappear with a cheerful, "No worries."

Gollums

It feels very strange to stand so many times at the edge of a stunning beach and not be able to go swimming. It is bakingly hot, the sky is ridiculously blue, the water dances and sparkles, but we daren't even put our feet in.

When we go to Elim Sands, however, there is no choice, so we take our lives in our hands and wade through the water.

It is worth it because we have made a long detour to see this famous sight. It is where the land meets the water just north of Cooktown, and the sandy cliffs are a riot of pinks, golds, reds and purples. Having come all this way to see it, we really ought to walk the length of the beach and inspect it properly, close up.

But at Elim Sands there is only a sliver of sand and that means we need to wade through the water. Hmm. The blokes stride out, insisting confidently that there is no threat. Admittedly it is only ankle-deep, but all the croc warnings are clear that we should stay metres back from any beach, so Merren and I make quite sure that Arthur is between us and any hungry croc who might be eyeing us off for lunch. He is big, so he would keep one happy for a while. We do see a few logodiles, which make us jump and squint at them intently. But no crocs pounce.

Those cliffs are certainly very spectacular. Great stripes and streaks of colour, several metres high, stretch the length of the beach, a wall of colours that would fill a drag queen with envy. We ooh and aah, take our photos, decide we have done it, turn tail and make it back alive.

There is a different type of risk at the next place: Split Rock, near Old Laura. This area is the home of the Quinkans, spirits living among the rocks. There are paintings of them on three enormous cliff-face galleries here. These Quinkans came in both good ones, the Tamaras which are very tall and thin, and naughty ones, the Imjims, chunky little Gollums who will pop out and hurt you.

These great slabs of stone are covered in dozens of pictures of Quinkans, as well as snakes, dogs and echidnas. Who knows how old they are? They are just outlines in ochre, two-dimensional figures, but they are so alive, full of the power of the Aboriginal Dreamtime stories.

They are some of the most vivid and dramatic rock art we have seen anywhere in Australia. And we are there entirely alone. The last time I stood in front of these magical paintings I was 24 years old. I have remembered them distinctly all this time and to see them again, just as I pictured them, after I have lived most of my life in between, gives me a surreal feeling.

Old Laura Homestead, just down the road, is a perfect example of an old grazing station. Because of the vast distances and the weather isolating the property for months on end, an Outback station like this had to be a little village. There was the large main house, surrounded by buildings for the blacksmith, the butcher, the meat house and the stockmen.

The daughters of the house, dressed in white muslin, were a big drawcard for the local society, which was mostly young men, and there were dances and parties. People rode long distances to get to the balls and stayed for days. This was all around 1900. There must have been a constant buzz of activity. Now Old Laura is abandoned, and a local group maintains it as an historic attraction.

Enough of history. We want to see birds and crocs.

The day is turning into a competition for the biggest of everything.

"Look at that palm tree," we exclaim, craning our necks up to see the raffish top of it, far above.

"What about that paperbark," we call, looking at a monster growing calmly on the edge of a lagoon, with a base the size of a small car.

"Have you ever seen so many mangoes?" we ask, looking up into a tree 100 years old, loaded with green fruit.

We have come into Lakefield National Park, and it is delivering the goods. Next stop is a lagoon down a track, covered in white water lilies. Up the road there are proper tourist attractions, Red Lily Lagoon and White Lily Lagoon. There are boardwalks and interpretive signs, and everyone stops there. Disappointingly, they are covered in weed this year, hardly a lily to be seen. But here in our little backwater lagoon, there is an absolute carpet of perky little lilies from bank to bank, looking crisp and delicate as they wave their white heads around like tiny ballerinas.

We are admiring them and exclaiming about how cute they are when Stuart suddenly stiffens and points. On the far side, half in and half out of the water is a monster croc, reclining on the muddy bank. We can only see half of him, but that's enough to frighten the wits out of anyone. He must be at least four metres, probably closer to five. We had been jokingly trying to entice a croc to show itself by throwing out insults like, "Ha, there aren't any crocs here." But when we see this terrifying creature, we fall silent. It has been a big day of big things.

THE OTT

What can you use an empty tuna tin for? We discover a brand-new application when we pop out of Lakefield National Park and into Moreton Telegraph Station. In the 1880s someone drew a dotted line up Cape York to The Tip. Then they put a telegraph line along it, the Overland Telegraph Track. Sound simple? It is hard to imagine the hardship this team of men must have endured as they battled to connect Australia to the world.

Fighting their way through jungle, enduring the exhausting heat and monsoonal rain, facing snakes and crocodiles, across this enormous distance, they struggled through and laid that telegraph line. Moreton and Musgrave Telegraph Stations along the way remain as relics of those days, with big airy buildings and huge old trees.

Now these places are buzzing with activity as 4-wheel-drive vehicles, coated with red dirt, pull in to camp. They are two of the rare places to stop and fuel up along the way, a mecca for road-weary travellers. Rough and ready, but so is everything up here. The luxury is some green grass and a cool drink to buy. We stop to have lunch and find a spot under a shady tree.

The blokes, of course, inspect the vehicles, the tyres, the… what's this? Arthur has lost a hub cab from his camper trailer. Not a big, flashy sports car city-type hub cap. Just a little thing about the size of a…

"How about a tuna tin?" suggests Merren. The conversation goes on.

"No, that won't work. Hang on, let's try it, it would just need a snip here and there."

It turns into a group effort. Between us we have a tin-opener that will take off the little rim, the tin snips to cut some tiny nips in it, the duct tape to bind it on. The men tap and poke it into place and confer with each other as they make minor adjustments.

We are standing back admiring the finished effect and wondering if it will actually work when someone walks by. He stops, comes back for a better look. "You'll probably only get about 50,000 kilometres out of that," he says, laughing. "You'll need to change your tyres before you need to get a new one."

This is the start of the Old Telegraph Track, or the OTT as it is nonchalantly called by everyone who wants to travel that route, the people with winches on their vehicles and a roof-rack loaded with spare tyres. (If you are towing a normal beach holiday type caravan you don't call it anything, you just shudder at the mention of it.) For a hundred years the OTT was the only road up to The Tip.

Then they built the Bamaga Road. Now you have a choice. The OTT is just a track, following a ruler-straight dotted line on the map. Remember the CREB Track? Maybe the engineer followed the same instructions: "Just bulldoze it direct from A to B, no worries." It is never graded, so it is rutted and rugged with deep sandy patches, several creek crossings and a maximum speed something like pushing a wheelbarrow. The Bamaga Road is wide and flat, but with teeth-rattling corrugations and choking clouds of dust, as the hoons fly past at full speed.

Q: Which route are we going to take?

A: The OTT, obviously

The track is quiet, the jungle scenery is lovely, and the creek crossings are So Much Fun. There are no crocs, they don't like the rocky terrain, so we can safely splash through the water, checking the depth, the holes in the rocks, the gradient up the other side.

We take videos on our phones of each other going through. The blokes spot each other through the risky sections with the two-way radios. On one crossing a girl from another vehicle stands in a deep hole to mark it for us. Most of the crossings have a group of people standing on the river bank, watching. There is great good humour and an esprit de corps among everyone.

Gunshot is the most famous of all because it is the wildest. Drivers have a choice at this crossing. There is one fairly tricky slope in, and three other almost vertical entries into the water. The daredevils crash down the steepest—nose first, rear bumper-bar pointed skywards—and make it out

pouring muddy water, to the cheers of their mates.

Sometimes they just crash down and that's it. On a previous time at Gunshot Ren spent an hour helping to dig out a Jeep standing on its nose at the bottom. We take the chicken track (the crossing that's tricky but not crazy) around Gunshot, but double back to have a look at the action. Not for us, thank you, it is exciting enough just watching. And it is dangerous—just a week ago someone died of a broken neck here.

One evening, at the end of a long day, we pop out of the challenges of the OTT into a little paradise, a series of waterfalls. The first one, Fruit Bat Falls, is perfect for swimming, with crystal-clear water falling from a wide flat ledge into a horseshoe-shaped pool. It would be the best resort swimming pool ever designed. We dive in and luxuriate under the falls as the water pounds our shoulders and froths around us. Just up the road are more: Elliott Falls, The Saucepan and Twin Falls. After the dust of the track they are totally blissful.

We stay the night, and plan to dive back onto the OTT next day. But, always expect the unexpected up here; the bush telegraph tells us that the track ahead is closed due to bushfires and we will have to go another way.

THE TIP

We have just driven from London to the middle of Russia. Well, you know what I mean—Sydney to The Tip. It has taken six weeks and 7,000 kilometres but we have finally made it to the very top of Australia. The Tip, as it is called, the pointy Land's End at the extremity of Cape York. It is the most northerly point of the Australian mainland.

Between here and New Guinea there are actually 300 Australian islands, sprinkled across the Torres Strait, mostly without water and very sparsely inhabited. One of these, Bogai, is only five kilometres from the coast of New Guinea.

But this rocky spit of land is the most northerly place you can stand on the actual continent and it is the place that draws the red dirt pilgrims. And this is the day we get there.

From where we are camped there is a seven-kilometre drive along a dusty track, then a 15-minute walk to get there. We leave the cars and trail around the sand to finally clamber over a rocky headland. It leads down to a simple little sign on a post: "You are Standing on the Northernmost Point of the Australian Mainland."

The place is buzzing with a couple of dozen people, posing beside the sign, taking turns for selfies and offering to take group photos. "I've been wanting to do this for 40 years," Arthur says, with a huge grin on his face. Everyone else is the same, they are all laughing and excited to be there, elated to have made it to The Tip.

L to R: Arthur, Merren, Nonie, Stuart, Maggie, Ren

Just being there is the point of it, if you will excuse the pun. Standing on that rocky outcrop with the Arafura Sea on one side and the Coral Sea on the other, looking north towards the Equator, with the vast Australian land mass behind you.

But apart from the iconic sense of being at The Tip, it is also supremely beautiful. As if those little green islands dotted to the horizon in every direction were not enough like the illustrations in a picture book, the sea is an incredible blue. We stare out at it, trying to decide the correct name for that exquisite colour. Finally, not really surprisingly, we decide it is aquamarine.

Of course, Arthur decides to throw a line in. He is obsessed with fishing, and this will be a place to remember. He and Stuart get out the fishing rods and start to cast. One gets away from Arthur, and another. He casts again. By now he has gathered an audience of men and little boys, standing around in an interested circle.

Suddenly he gets a tug on the line and pulls in a good sized Queenfish. Arthur and Stuart take the hook out and pose for a photo: that picture is going to go straight to the poolroom. Then they throw it back and it blasts away.

There is a man in a tinny motoring back and forth near the shore. What is he doing, we wonder. Then a Torres Strait Islander woman walks down to the water's edge, and he comes in to pick her up. She steps on board with the confidence of a lifetime around boats, and they speed away to one of those islands.

"What a lifestyle," we muse, envying the idea of living in this heavenly place, with fish and coconuts there for the taking, and all the time in the world to relax and enjoy every day.

Of course, there is no perfect Paradise. When we had arrived at the little parking lot at The Tip, just a dusty circle at the end of the track, we discovered that the authorities have not caught up with the number of travellers arriving every day. There are no facilities, no rubbish management. The parking area is indeed a tip. Arthur springs into life as soon as he can ask Dr Google who the responsible local Councils and Members of Parliament are.

He puts a post on the Cape York Facebook page, and finds he has lit a match and started a bushfire. The post is rushed with likes and comments, lots of applause. He talks to people about it, and they say, "Are you the guy who put that post on Facebook?" Tourist operators congratulate him. "Good on ya," they say. "Hammer them." I can see that we are going to have to come back to check on progress in a year or two. When they build that dunny they really should name it after Arthur.

Not the Frenchman's Track

When one wheel of your vehicle nearly falls into a deep hole as you are fording a rocky creek, and you are alone and far from help, it tends to stick in your mind. We have remembered the Not the Frenchman's Track very clearly for seven years because of that.

We had been looking for a route to get to the coast called the Frenchman's Track, but we met some people who had abandoned a trailer with a broken leaf spring, on the track. They were two families with a bunch of grubby, happy kids. The adults were grimly cheerful in an exhausted sort of way and were clearly not friends with the Frenchman's. They told us the track was a trailer-killer, so we backed out of that idea.

We saw another dotted line on the map further south and found ourselves on this track instead. We have called it the "Not the Frenchman's Track" ever since. It was very challenging and very memorable.

There was a winching moment that first time, up a steep sandy pinch. We got out of that with a well-placed tree to winch onto. And then there was a heart-stopping moment at the Wenlock River when one wheel hung perilously over a hole in the rocks as we madly threw logs in to give us enough purchase to inch out rather than fall in and be wedged inextricably.

So obviously you can see why we wanted to go back to the Not the Frenchman's again. Can you? Hmm. This time, we have backup. Three vehicles to spot each other through the tricky bits and to take videos of all the exciting moments.

It is a blissful track, narrow, sandy, winding, and with changes in vegetation at every turn. A patch of light shining on bright green trees with delicate leaves makes way for a stand of a thousand spindly paperbarks. There is a little forest of grass trees, looking like a group of skinny people with crazy hair. There are pandanus palms and grevilleas.

We crawl along at less than walking pace, navigating the ruts and washouts and stopping to take photographs. When we come to the Wenlock River it is just the same as we remembered—a broad expanse of dry sand at this time of year, dotted with trees, with a rocky water crossing about 30 metres ahead.

Those broad patches of rocks are where we almost came unstuck last time. It is still vivid in our minds, and it still looks very alarming. The rocks are lumpy and bumpy, with lots of holes and ridges. We pick our way gingerly over it, looking at the hazards and picking the best line. To our amazement Ren and I see the biggest of the logs we had pushed into that almost-disastrous hole, still wedged in it all these years later.

Stuart guides Ren through first. The car crawls with extreme caution over the rocks, skirting the holes, and through the water to the other side. Ren crosses back on foot to me, hopping from rock to rock. Arthur creeps safely through next.

When everyone else is on the far bank Ren and I start to walk across, picking our way over the rocky stepping stones. In the middle of the crossing I can't quite reach the next foothold. "Don't put your foot there," says Ren, pointing to a thick mat of slimy leaves and sticks in the water.

But I miss my footing, step down onto it, and drop into deep, mucky, murky water. I am in a frighteningly creepy mass of leaf and stick in a deep, dark hole, with nothing to step onto and nothing to grab to pull myself out.

Luckily Ren had taken the camera as a precaution (I have form with this sort of thing). He reaches down to pull me up but, "Save the camera," I call. (I forgot about the two-way radio handset in my back pocket—oops). I thrash about, grabbing for anything to give me some leverage, gasping with fear and expecting any second to find myself kicking a crocodile in the head. There is nothing to step on, nothing to hold.

Then Ren yanks me up and I finally make it out, covered in leaf litter and muck, and flop back fully dressed into a pool of clear water to rinse off. Just for a moment, crocs be damned, it can't be any more risky than it just was. The others, having realised we were a lot longer than expected, have wandered back down to the riverbank and are busy taking photos and laughing. I think I might have just used one more of my nine lives.

After that the next crossing at the Pascoe River crossing is very tame, a pretty, shallow ford with sand and pebbles. We are looking for somewhere to camp near the river. It is time to stop, even though we have taken almost all day to travel 25 kilometres. Ren takes a little walk to see if he can find a spot.

When he comes back he is accompanied by a wiry bushman, Beau. "You would be welcome to stay in my clearing," Beau offers graciously. We are very happy to accept. We wouldn't be able to go on anyway, even if we wanted to; there is a young Aboriginal man and woman there as well, friends of Beau. Apparently they have bogged their car and it is blocking the track up ahead.

If you are worried about your mortgage, Beau has a solution. His home is ultra-minimalist, just a tarpaulin strung across some poles. He doesn't look as if he needs much. No shoes, for one thing, and no comb. No worries about security, so no locks—oh wait…no doors.

"Where do you go in The Wet?" I ask. "I wait till the river gets up to my place," he says. He points to a spot at the front of his campsite, 30 metres above the current water level. "Then I go to higher ground till the river goes down again."

"The water reaches so high!" I exclaim. "Yeah," he says. "Sometimes it goes right over the roof there. If you only own enough so it fits in one packing chest it's not a problem. I just tie it to a tree on a couple of 44-gallon drums with a long rope and let it float up with the water while I'm away."

Ren and Stuart go and pull the young couple's car out, then Beau and his friends go off together. He has a bag slung over his shoulder, so we assume he is away for the night, leaving us camped in his little clearing, having a paddle in the shallow water of the rocky creek crossing and listening to the squawking of a Great Palm Cockatoo in the trees.

Lockhart Art

What is the best place to buy authentic Aboriginal Art? Where it is painted, of course.

Nonie and Stuart have fallen in love with Aboriginal Art. They spent a week last year volunteering at Yuendumu, a famous Indigenous art centre in the Red Centre of the country, and now they have their eye on the art centre at Lockhart on the coast nearby. So we spear off towards it, pop out of the track and cross the Great Dividing Range once more, heading towards the coast.

Our quest is Lockhart, an Aboriginal Community. There used to be a mission nearby where the Indigenous people were taken when white settlement came to this area, but times have now changed, and Native Title has given great tracts of land back to the First Nations people all over Australia. In this area, the Aboriginal people came back to Lockhart, which had been their homeland, back to "Country."

This is a dry community. No alcohol is sold here, and visitors cannot carry any unless they are travelling through. In quite a lot of Aboriginal communities all over the Outback a total ban on alcohol has been legislated, mainly at the request of the women, who suffered the worst effects of alcohol abuse in their families.

Dry communities have had a dramatic effect on the health and wellbeing of the places where it has been introduced. Kids are fed and sent to school more and women can live with less domestic violence.

One of the very positive outcomes in a number of communities is the development of art centres. Local Indigenous people are creating dramatic and unique art which is now bringing in big money overseas. And in these communities, it is possible to see piles of them at local prices. The artists get 50% of the sale price, the art centre gets the other 50% and uses it to fund paint, materials, workshops, and trips to visit galleries. One artist has just come back from Paris, another one recently had an exhibition in Singapore.

When we get to the art centre, there are two women sitting outside. "These are the artists," the manager tells us. Two of them anyway, it seems to be a centre for a lot of local artists, but these are the ones who are painting here today. Inside there are artworks in many styles, some traditional, some modern.

They are all acrylic on canvas and they are piled on tables, spread out on the floor, and hanging on the walls. Our friends are eagerly looking through the heaps of paintings with the intention to buy something.

Ren and I sit on the veranda with the women, chatting. They are Evelyn Omeenyo and Thelma Hobson. Friendly and relaxed, they talk about how they take the kids down to the beach and out to the hills, to pass on the old traditions.

The men teach the boys how to make spears and stone axes, how to hunt for game, how to find the gum they need to fix a stone axe-head to a handle. The women show the girls how to find bush tucker, the way to wrap the prickly pandanus leaves in a roll of soft paperbark to carry back to camp, and how to weave their finely knotted dilly bags.

Evelyn mentions a trip she had with a group of artists to Sydney and Canberra. I look at her again. She looks familiar somehow, can it be possible that I recognise her?

"Were you in the paper?" I ask.

She gives a giggle, "Yes, I was there to show my weaving techniques, now some of my work is in the Parliament House."

"I thought so!" I exclaim. "I read an article about you in the newspaper."

Evelyn tells us about her childhood on the mission, and how her family took her away to Bamaga to get an education. She came back to the mission to live as an adult, but then it was closed down and this little township was built at Lockhart instead.

"It was 1972. There were three of us left at the mission who didn't want to leave. One old lady, she was refusing to go. So they sent the navy. They just came and put lifejackets on us. The old lady was throwing rocks at them. But when those lifejackets were on us there was nothing more to do, they just took us and brought us here.

"This is my tribal area, but I was born on the mission land so that was home to me. But they built the community here. Our men came in and cleared it, and then a carpenter started to build the houses. I was working then, in the hospital here. My kids are in Cairns, but my grandson is here now with me. "

Evelyn is a white-haired old woman now. She has lived so much of the troubled recent history of the Indigenous people after white settlement in their ancestral lands—dispossession, death and poverty—and has survived it with grace and a sense of humour.

After a while she gets restless. Our friends have all bought paintings and it is time to go. "Now I'm hungry," she says, dismissing us. But as we leave, I look in the workroom. Both of the women are back in there bending over a workbench, with paintbrushes.

Chilli Beach

We saw something extraordinary the last time we were at Chilli Beach, and it has been etched in our memory ever since. It was enough to bring us back, with our friends in tow, in the hope of seeing it again. And enough for us not to talk about it, in case it didn't happen again.

So we head for Chilli Beach, past the Lockhart River and up the coast a bit. These little Pacific Ocean gems would be enough to bring anyone here just for the sweet scenery—beaches with curving swathes of fine white sand, lined with swaying coconut palms and edged with a brilliant blue sea.

Of course, you can't swim here, such a pity, but apart from that—perfect! And Chilli Beach has a special beauty, with a tiny island just off the shore, placed there for the best possible effect, a pretty little bump with strips of sand and a few palm trees.

The whole scene is really over the top. If it was a Hollywood movie you would say, "Come on, Leonardo Di Caprio, that's too much, cut it back a bit, a set like that is unbelievable." But it is real, and it is truly lovely.

There is another island at the north end of the beach which had an interesting moment in history. When the Mutiny on the Bounty in 1789 meant that Captain Bligh was put into an open boat with a few sailors and told, "Row, you bastard," it started a dramatic story that has taken on a life of its own ever since, with books and movies retelling the improbable tale of survival.

After rowing across the open ocean, and making it against impossible odds, Bligh and his little group of sailors first made landfall here and called it Restoration Island.

But we are not here for history, we are here to watch nature give us a show. As the sun starts to get lower in the sky, just on dusk, we sit on the beach and wait. And gradually something magical happens, just as we had hoped. A few tiny black birds come winging in towards the island—Metallic Starlings. Then another little group flies in, perhaps a dozen or so. And another.

Over the next half hour hundreds of thousands of those tiny birds fly in and merge into one swooping, sweeping mass. They fly one way, then abruptly swerve, swing back in a flowing wave, one huge cloud of countless tiny birds. Every few minutes more keep arriving to join the flock. It is utterly spellbinding. How many birds are there? How do they know to turn on a dime like that, the instantaneous reverse, swing, drop, climb, and swing back again? It is a wonder of nature. "You would never tire of watching that," says Arthur quietly, transfixed by the sight. We all are.

As the sun drops abruptly below the horizon and the sky darkens, the show is suddenly over. With a few last flips and swoops, they all settle for the night on that little island. The next day they leave for wherever they go, and then return to do it all once more, and again, every day. It was spellbinding, astounding. And we were the only people there watching it.

As we turn from the beach, Ren and I high five. It really did happen again, just as we had hoped, and we were able to show something truly amazing to our friends.

Drongos

After that heart-stopping experience, you can see the excitement is not all about crocodiles up here. There is also incredible birdlife. Not just the red-winged whatnot or the crested thingummy. There are absolutely captivating birds everywhere. Like the brolgas, for example, elegant grey storks who mate for life and always travel in pairs, gracefully lifting off the grass together and flying casually away.

Or the spectacular Jabiru cranes, with long fearsome-looking beaks, shiny black feathers and red legs, that stand, a metre high, at the edge of lagoons. And the majestic wedge-tailed eagles, with a wingspan of up to two metres, that stay feasting on road-kill till the very last moment, then heave reluctantly into the air.

I'm not much of a bird-watcher, I can never see them. "Look," they say, pointing to the top of a tree. "Isn't it beautiful!" All I see is leaves waving. I prefer to look at hawks, big and brown, wheeling in slow-motion circles in the open sky, and easy to spot.

But Stuart has the eyesight of a wild animal. He could pick a lizard at a hundred paces and he sees birds everywhere. So when we pull in at Artemis station he is very happy when the owner, Sue Shephard, invites us to come on a bird walk next morning. "I've got some feeders out, we usually see some," she says.

Next morning at first light we front up and are joined by five other people: "Bob's Birdwatching Tours." Bob has a big hat and a roll-your-own cigarette. His four clients are equipped with no-nonsense binoculars and sensible shoes. One of the men has a camera with a lens the size of a small child.

We wander off into the bush, trailing along behind Sue and Bob. They talk to us all in hushed tones. It is hard to hear what they are saying but clearly Sue knows all the places to find the birds. I think maybe she even knows every individual bird. She is trying to reinstate the birdlife to the way it was 100 years ago by careful management of habitat and feeding.

"There's a spangled drongo," she says. The camera shutters rattle, everyone peers at the tree. I can't see it but, "I know all about drongos," I mutter to myself, "I've worked with a lot of them in my time."

"Anyone seeing those finches?" asks one of the women.

"Yes," the others all chorus. I did see a few small blurry things flash past.

"There's a cuckoo shrike," Bob says.

"That's a mature female," Sue adds. "And there's a juvenile male."

But the endangered Golden-shouldered Parrot is our real quarry, the reason Bob and his group are here. Sue calls them the Ant-bed Parrot, because they drill a hole in the termite mounds and lay their eggs there.

"The mother raises the chicks usually. But I saw a father bird rear his chicks once, after the mother died," she says fondly. "Seven of them. And sometimes a male will help a female raise chicks that are not his own, in the hopes that after they are grown she might be willing to go another round with him, and he would get some offspring."

Of course Sue finds some Golden-shouldered Parrots. The binoculars go up, and the cameras click. Everyone is happy, it has been a good morning's work. And I have had a nice walk in the bush.

We are heading towards Normanton and the Gulf of Carpentaria. We sadly waved Merren and Arthur off at Musgrave Station, giving them both a gold star for achievement. Arthur can now tackle any reasonably awful track, and Merren saves, "Oh S**t!" for those moments that really deserve it. (Learning which is which is a fine art.)

One of the nice things about being in the Outback is how helpful people are, how friendly and, usually with few words, how welcoming. Many times, if we just can't find anywhere to camp, we have driven up to a station homestead and asked if we can stay somewhere on the property. We have never been refused, it is always just a polite, "No dogs or guns, and no fires."

So it comes as a shock to suddenly come across something really different. This is a back country stretch of the Burke Developmental Road with virtually no traffic and lots of nice-looking places to stop for the night.

But all along the way are large, new-looking signs that scream at the traveller, "No Camping, No Fishing, No Shooting. If you leave the road you will be trespassing, and the police will prosecute. Police patrol this area." They are big signs full of this extraordinary stuff and decorated with Queensland Police badges and Neighbourhood Watch insignia.

We pass one, then another, and another. There are so many spots where we would normally just pull off the road and camp, but the signs are very aggressive, and we are law-abiding types. So we head for the main station, to ask permission. No chance, Charlie—the No Entry sign at the front gate even says, "No water." Outrageous—whoever heard of people being denied water way out here if they need it?

It gets later and later, and darkness is falling. It has been a long day and the drivers are getting very tired. The road ahead is filling up with little wallabies, just waiting to be knocked down. Eventually Nonie calls through on the two-way, "This is ridiculous, it isn't safe, we should just camp here anyway."

So we do, exclaiming about how shocking those signs are, and how we would relish the conversation with anyone who came to bail us up and threaten us with prosecution. Bring it on. I fantasise about spray-painting RESIST over those signs. Nonie's suggested wording is unprintable.

Emerald Water

Gotta love the simple life. It doesn't get much simpler than this: Wake up. Eat. Drive. Sleep.

How about this for a perfect example of the simple life and its simple pleasures. We stop in Karumba, in a caravan park, and because there is an actual toaster there we can all have actual toast and honey for breakfast. What a rare treat!

So there we are, coffee in one hand, toast in the other, and just a few metres away is a little brolga family. Mum, Dad and child, having their breakfast too, pecking away in the dust. I make a little clicking noise, and the brolga I am watching looks up and blinks at me. Just that, but I'm ridiculously thrilled. I just communicated with an actual brolga! We had a moment together, that brolga and me! Up close and personal!

So that leads us into thinking about happiness. This morning some politician is waking up furious, the man who made those mean-spirited signs on the road is waking up angry, Donald Trump is waking up, well, Donald Trump. But the four of us are sitting looking at the ocean, cheerfully munching our toast and honey, and me all goofy about my new BFF, the brolga…yep, it's all good.

We are in Karumba, on the Gulf of Carpentaria. It is a tiny dot on the map that draws people who like to fish, and people who like to sit with a beer and watch the famous sunset. We choose the sunset and settle in to watch the show. It gets its spectacular effect because the sun sets over the water here. It is so different to what we are used to on the East Coast.

The sun slides slowly down then drops abruptly below the long horizon, lighting up the ocean in a blaze of red. But that is far from the end of it. For the next half hour the colour gets more and more intense, spreading across the mud flats, painting them with changing swathes and stripes of crimson and orange. Can you take too many pictures of sunsets?

We are here because we have had another mechanical moment with our camper trailer. The bearing on the other side has decided to collapse. So we had stopped, set up our camp chairs beside the road and settled in for the long wait for a tow truck. Several hours later it arrived.

The towie, Ron, is a man of few words. He ambles silently over, tips his hat back and gives the camper a long stare. Then he loads it up and takes it into Karumba, and there it sits during the long wait for a spare

part to arrive. If you are in a hurry this far from anywhere, you are in the wrong place.

How to fill in a few days? There is a famous gorge, Lawn Hill, not far south. Not far in Outback terms, that is—only 500 kilometres. So a day later we roll in and set up in one of the tents there.

Lawn Hill (Boodjimulla National Park) attracts tourists because of its long, thin, winding gorge with bright emerald water. It seems to have established itself as a must-see spot on the grey nomad itineraries. A little electric boat does brisk business going up and down the gorge, full of tour groups with grey hair and name tags.

We decide to take a couple of the walking tracks instead, following the dotted lines on a little map. It is hot and steep and stony, but the views from the top are absolutely worth the effort, to look down the ribbon of vivid green water, framed by red rock walls, snaking off into the distance. It is completely silent, and we are alone up there.

After a while we clamber down to a pool at the bottom and sit under the Indarri Falls, the water pounding down like a natural spa. The water is a perfect temperature and the only crocs to be found in the area are freshies.

That is all very lovely, and we are very glad to have finally made it to Lawn Hill, after passing by it several times on our way north, or south, or east, but I am much more excited about another local point of interest, a place I have wanted to visit for more than 40 years. In 1976, a team from the Australian Museum started to excavate a 30-million-year-old prehistoric site at Riversleigh.

What they discovered was an area rich with the fossilised remains of three-metre-high flightless birds, prehistoric lions with retractable claws, monster wombats, crocodiles that could climb trees, huge kangaroos with teeth so large they are nicknamed Fangaroo, snapping turtles, and thylacines like the Tassie Tiger.

At Riversleigh, there is one corner where the public can catch a glimpse of this ferocious wildlife, captured in the rocks. Of course, it is not very popular with tourists—it is a long way down a rough road and only nerds would want to go, but I am truly excited about it.

We get out at a little windswept parking bay. There is an information board, and a path leading up to a rocky hill. Here and there are small signs explaining what we are looking at: a cross-section of the shell of a huge turtle; the top of the leg of a massive crocodile. We turn a corner, and there in front of us, perfectly clear in the rock, is the thigh bone of Big Bird, white against the red rock.

If you are getting a bit full of yourself, a trip to the Outback will settle you right back. First, there is the sky at night. That huge bowl of a gazillion stars makes you feel very insignificant.

And then looking at things 30 million years old (or 250 million, or 500) will make you realise that your life is as brief and unimportant as a single-celled organism in a prehistoric sea, or a cockroach walking the earth at the time of the dinosaurs, or even a Big Bird here at Riversleigh. Let's face it, that mighty creature once stomped around terrorising the neighbourhood, but all that is left now is a bit of its leg bone, fossilised in a rock.

PART VI

Arnhem Land and The Top End

Jurassic Park

If we had a dollar for every time someone has said to us, "Aren't you scared camping out there in the bush," we would be rolling in money. We do camp in the bush almost every night, completely isolated. But in a minute flat I could count fifty ways we would be more likely to get into a dangerous situation.

Just occasionally, however, there is a moment that lifts the heart rate a bit. A few years ago, camping in the bush south of Darwin, we discovered that there was an actual axe-murderer hiding out somewhere nearby. We found this out by emerging from the scrub and finding ourselves face-to-face with a roadblock manned by serious-looking soldiers with sub-machine guns. The guy had decapitated a man down south and hightailed it up here to hide out somewhere in the vicinity of our peaceful campsite.

But apart from that surreal moment there has never been a problem.

So tonight we are happily camped at a lookout with a Steven Spielberg view. If you have seen Jurassic park, this is it. The plain, way down below, spreads across to the far distance, dotted with trees and patches of grassland. It is a spectacular view and there definitely should be dinosaurs down there.

We are sitting after dinner, enjoying a movie on the iPad under the stars, when a vehicle comes by. Two cars have gone past over the last few hours and disappeared down the road. But this one pauses, backs up and turns, with the motor still running and its lights on high beam trained directly at us. We wait, but they don't move off.

Ren gets up. "Turn off your headlamp," he says. "Go inside, close the door and zip up."

"Get me the satellite phone," I say. He hands it to me. "Just dial Triple O if you need to."

I hold it up while it searches for the satellite and connects, watching Ren walk across. After a while he comes back. Of course, as usual, there is no problem at all. They are just a few young blokes looking for a camping spot for the night.

We are 114 kilometres in on the road to the furthest corner of Arnhem Land. That is the square bit right at the top on the map of Australia. And way up there, in the north-eastern corner, is a little place called Nhulunbuy. Someone I knew as a child became a teacher here. The name has stuck in my mind ever since, and I really want to see it.

It is quite a long way, 670 kilometres, and there is only one probably very dreary road in, the Arnhem Highway. (That word highway, as I am sure you are starting to realise, is often rather misleading in Australia—it just means the main way to get from one state to the next and can be any standard from multi-lane bitumen to bone-crunching goat track.)

But we are going, no matter what. To get there, first we have to go to Hell's Gate. It really deserved its name in the early days. The explorers and gold prospectors, back in the 1800s would gather at a big outcrop of rock near the town, ready to brave the wilds together, and the saying was that most never returned. They died of many things, not least spears from the local Indigenous people who, not surprisingly, didn't fancy all these Europeans invading their homeland.

The Hell's Gate roadhouse was pretty rough when we were last here seven years ago. It looked as if nothing much had changed for a hundred years or so, possibly not even the tea towels. But now, what the hell has happened to Hell's Gate? At the entrance is a hand painted sign saying, "There are no Strangers Here, Only People You Haven't Met Yet."

And inside the building everything has been redecorated, and is painted and fresh, backcountry chic. New Management evidently. It is very nice, full marks for effort and A for attitude, but I can't help feeling that there is something appealing about a daggy old roadhouse. When you are that far from civilisation it really should look like it.

We pass through Hell's Gate and travel past Borroloola, where the main tourist attraction is the boat ramp. (No, that's unfair, as well as the boat ramp there is a very occasional weird massive cloud formation called the Morning Glory that rolls in from the ocean in the early morning. There's no end to the excitement in Borroloola.)

Then on to Daly Waters with its definitely unrenovated buildings.

Then a stretch of the Stuart Highway going north. Finally, we strike out to the north-east, into Arnhem Land at last. Of course it will be flat and arid and featureless, a long expanse of not much.

That is what we expect but it turns out to be big surprise. Parts of it are hilly and lots of it is forest. There are spectacular groves of grass trees and prehistoric-looking cycads, brilliant green with the sun shining through their spiky fronds. A buffalo with horns two metres wide runs across the road. A herd of wild donkeys turns to look as we drive past. It is a long, long way, but it is such an interesting drive in that constantly-changing landscape.

We are looking for a place to get off the road for lunch. Red dust all over your sandwiches from a passing vehicle kind of spoils the taste.

So we turn down a track to Barrapunta Outstation. At the end of the dirt track there is a cluster of buildings that looks like an Aboriginal community. It is private property, obviously, so we'll just go on to find somewhere to turn around. An Indigenous man wanders over to us.

"We were just looking for somewhere to have our lunch," we say.

"No worries, mate. Go and talk to Kiwi Ian," he replies with a smile.

There is a radio playing and the smell of fresh paint in one of the stone buildings nearby. Kiwi Ian emerges. He is a chunky New Zealander with a laid-back air. Ian is restoring the stone buildings to turn the place into a ranger station and the Traditional Owner in the area is keen to encourage tourists.

We get a guided tour, down to the little creek with crystal-clear water, past the array of solar-powered batteries. "We'll be ready before The Wet," Ian says confidently. Like so many people up here, he came for a few weeks and has stayed for years.

When we get to Nhulunbuy, it is a very big shock. All these years I have imagined a shabby outpost way up here at the end of the track, with just a few dilapidated sheds and shacks. Instead there are green lawns and neat buildings. There is a crisply-painted Yacht Club with a dozen boats bobbing nearby. The insignia on the sign is two crocodiles—maybe the message is, "Don't Fall Overboard."

And there is even a Surf Lifesaving Club. Surf is a bit of an overstatement for those gently lapping waves, but sometimes when the ocean is clear enough they open one of the beaches and have croc spotters watching out while people swim.

Nhulunbuy is the centre for the whole vast area of Arnhem Land. Most of it is Aboriginal Land, and people live in communities dotted across the map. The first night we are here, there is a big party on the beach nearby, with age-old songs and clapping sticks going on till dawn.

As in so many places it was mining money that made this town into the neat place it is: Rio Tinto and Alcan, mining bauxite. But it hasn't all been good. The smelter finally closed down in 2014 and 1200 jobs disappeared overnight.

We go to sightsee along the exquisite beaches, long stretches of white sand with stunning azure blue water. Of course, you can't swim, but what is that in the water over there? Not people, surely. Yes, it is two Aboriginal men fishing with spears, up to their knees in water and well out from the beach.

They come in with a fish on the prongs of a spear. The women under the trees are cooking them over a little fire. "Just out of the water," calls one, smiling as she takes another mouthful. The picture could have been any time in the last 60,000 years.

We ask Benjamin, one of the men, "Aren't you afraid of the crocodiles?" He smiles. "We just think of the fish."

What a Croc!

The Top End might be part of Australia, but it's a different country.

Things people say to you, just for starters.

"We were fishin' and I dropped me rod. There were a couple of salties around, so we fired a shot into the water to scare them away while I dived in and got it."

"Ya need three oars when you go fishin' off here. Two to row the boat and one to whack the barramundi back into the water."

The note on the door of a business: "I'm in the backyard, come round the side, the dog's chained up."

And the newspaper headlines are always a rich source of amusement. Just this morning, for instance: "Drunk Driver Smashes Car into Police Station. Sen-Sgt Mace said that they had been looking for a car which had been hooning around and doing burnouts. 'We were not able to find the vehicle,' she said. 'However the vehicle came to us.'"

The souvenir shops in the Top End even have a book consisting of nothing but a collection of the front pages of the regional newspaper, the Northern Territory News. This literary masterpiece is called "What a Croc!" The front cover features a photo of a young bloke in a tinny. He is leaping out of the way of a lunging crocodile. "G'day Bait," the headline quips.

The whole book is full of these gems. Oh, to be the sub-editor thinking up the witty puns that have made the Northern Territory News famous. Probably my favourite is, "Why I Stuck a Cracker Up My Clacker." Yes, right there on the front page of a capital city newspaper. If you are not Australian it is probably best if you translate this one for yourself.

And, of course, there are the people you meet. The Top End attracts a fair selection of people who are eccentric, or adventurous, or who just don't want to live a regular Down South shoe-wearing kind of life. There is quite a sprinkling of people who have left a past, or a marriage, behind. It's best not to ask too many questions. And never to ask a surname.

And then there are the tourists who come up here. There are plenty of organised tours to the famous places like Kakadu National Park, and good on them for getting out here and having a look. But off the beaten track you meet a great assortment of people whose main thing in common is not caring about being dusty, or who have a dislike for schedules, or four walls. You rub shoulders with all sorts of people, swapping travellers' tales and sharing hints.

Camping back at Nhulunbuy in Arnhem land, for example. On one side we had Cat, a doctor, and her husband Wayne, a businessman. Next to them were Aaron the plumber with a big ute and a big beard, and his wife Deniel. On the other side was Bill, who owns a prawn trawler off Townsville. It was a little picture of Australia right there. And six kids running around, barefoot, wiry and scraggly-haired, only standing still long enough to eat.

Now we are heading west to the Top End, popping into Darwin to have our vehicle serviced. It's just down the road—about 1000 kilometres. Back along the Arnhem Highway, with its violent corrugations and lovely scenery again, and onto the Stuart Highway. Mataranka is nearby, where Jeannie Gunn lived on Elsey Station in 1902 and later wrote the classic memoir "We of the Never-Never" that has given the Top End it's favourite tourism slogan: "You'll Never Never Know if you Never Never Go."

Until 1974 Darwin was a raffish town, more South-East Asian than European. At one stage there were more Chinese residents than whites, and the houses were flimsy, built on stilts to catch the breeze. Then on Christmas Eve 1974 Cyclone Tracy roared through, with winds of more than 200 kilometres per hour. No-one knows exactly how much wilder it was, because the force of the wind broke the recording equipment.

But the fury of that night flattened Darwin and changed it forever. When it was rebuilt, with sturdy cyclone-proof buildings, rather sadly it started to become a modern city. Sort of. It is still very small, relaxed and friendly. Everyone wears shorts and sandals, and the residents have a fierce pride in being different to the rest of Australia.

We have a week to kill here, so we tick off the tourist list: the Mindil Beach markets, looking for gifts and eating laksa; the Deckchair Cinema, watching a movie as the sun sets, with the palm trees swaying and the water lapping nearby.

We visit the Museum and Art Gallery, which has a stunning exhibition of a 10-year collaboration between a western and an Aboriginal artist, John Wolseley and Mulkun Wirrpanda. With both Western and Aboriginal art forms, it records the bush tucker from Arnhem land that Mulkun knew as a young woman so that the knowledge is not lost forever. It is breathtakingly beautiful.

Apart from that there is nothing much else we want to do in the heat but splash about in the Wave Pool, a fake beach on the harbour where you can swim in gentle surf without fear of being eaten.

Our car is waiting for a part to arrive from the UK, our camper trailer is in for repair, my old sandals have given up the ghost and even my $1 Australia Day thongs from the hardware store have finally broken. But with a tropical view of Darwin Harbour from our balcony and a cold drink in the fridge it's not a bad place to be stranded for a few days.

And then suddenly it is time to go home, 4,000 kilometres south. Would we like to come back to the desert, the sand dunes, and the vast landscapes and unique beauty of the Outback? To climb a sandhill and cross a creek. To stand at night under the limitless jet-black sky and gaze at the stars. To stare at a distant horizon with nothing at all in between. And to sit around a campfire with a glass of red and some good friends, swapping yarns and marvelling at our good luck in being there. Would we? Tomorrow would be good.

GLOSSARY OF TERMS: AUSTRALIAN ENGLISH

Akubra: Australian Outback hat, similar to a Stetson, made of felted rabbit fur

Beanie: a knit cap

BFF: Best Friend Forever

Bindi-eye: Painful spiky burr

Bloke: An Australian man

Cark it: Die

Chook: Hen

Corroboree: Indigenous ritual dance

Diggers: Army privates who dug trenches in World War I, now a general term for soldiers

Dunny: Slang for toilet

Dreamtime stories: Creation myths of the Aboriginal people

Drongo: Slang for a fool

Epi-pen: Device to inject epinephrine to shut down a severe allergic response

Finger buns: Sweet bun of soft dough with icing

Freshie: A freshwater crocodile

Grey nomad: Retirees who are travelling Australia with a caravan

Hammer it: Go fast and hard

Hit the turps: Drank a lot of alcohol

Hoons: Young men, layabouts, who "hoon around" in their cars

Kilometre: 0.62 miles (100km = 60 miles)

Knocked off: Stolen

Metre: 1.09 yards or 39.3 inches

Missus: Wife

Mug: Fool

Nerd: Geek

Paddock: A field, usually very large

Property: A farm or ranch, often enormous (interchangeable with station)

Pub: Local hotel, more for beer than accommodation

Rabbiting on: Talking

Roadhouse: Roadside servo stocking fuel, food, spare parts, basic groceries and souvenirs

RSL: Returned Services League Club

Servo: Fuel filling station (service station)

Shandy: Old-fashioned "ladies drink" made of half and half lemonade and beer.

Snorkel: Elevated air intake to enable a vehicle to cross creeks

Sod's Law: Also known as Murphy's Law—if something can go wrong it will go wrong

Station: A very large farm or ranch, sometimes as big as half a million acres (also see property)

Suss: Suspicious

Swaggie: Tramp

The Top End: The far north of the Northern Territory

The Wet: The wet season

Thongs: Not (ahem) an article of clothing, but rubber sandals, called flip-flops in most other countries

Tinny: A small aluminium boat powered by either oars or an outboard motor

Towie: Tow truck driver

Tradie: Tradesman

Triple O: The Australian emergency number

UHT milk: Milk that has been treated to give a long shelf life out of the refrigerator

Ute: A utility vehicle, a pickup truck

Yarn: A chat or a story

4 Wheel Drive or 4X4: Sports Utility Vehicle

ABOUT SAM MITCHELL

Remember the young man with the crazy solar-powered bike? We met him in the middle of the Canning Stock Route, near Lake Tobin. We wondered whether he would make it to the end, or have to abandon his attempt and be rescued, and we recalled him with some anxiety. To our relief and admiration we later discovered that he not only safely completed his adventure, but was named Australian Geographic Young Adventurer of the Year for 2017.

ABOUT THE AUTHOR

When we were 21 years old and married for six months we sold everything that wasn't nailed down and went to Africa. Our only plan was to get out of Australia, where we had grown up, and have an adventure. The cheapest way to get to another continent was by boat, and we grabbed the chance. Three weeks later we stood on a dock in South Africa without a clue about anything. We had a page torn out of an old school atlas as our guidebook and we learnt everything by trial and error, mostly error. We didn't go home for three years.

We travelled the length of Africa by penny buses and hitch-hiking, ending up going down the Nile on the deck of a barge. We roamed Europe on a motor-cycle. We got a taste for going to remote and difficult places and for living on the smell of an oily rag in order to explore yet another fascinating country.

We bought a beat-up old Land Rover in England and drove it home to Australia, living in the back and surviving one hair-raising event after another. We travelled Australia, crossing deserts, sand dunes and flooded rivers.

And then, of course, we settled down, raised a family and paid off the mortgage. But it was only a matter of time before we set off again…

MORE BOOKS BY MAGGIE RAMSAY

DESERT AND DUST DOWN UNDER

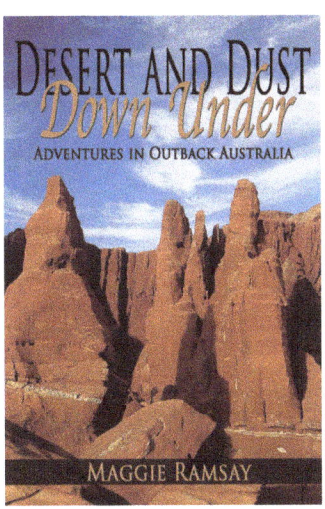

Do you love to travel? Desert and Dust Down Under will instantly take you on a fascinating journey across one of the strangest countries on earth. The spectacular scenery, the unique animals and the friendly, laid-back people of Outback Australia are amusing and entertaining. And there are plenty of surprises along the way. Written with a wry sense of humour, this adventure along back roads and rugged tracks is a great read whether you want to explore Down Under in person or from the comfort of your armchair.

Praise for Desert and Dust Down Under:
"Fantastic book. Really reading the book, I would look forward to reading more/similar type of books." Neil Grimley. 5 Stars. Reviewed on 4 May, 2017. Verified Purchase

The Italian Camino

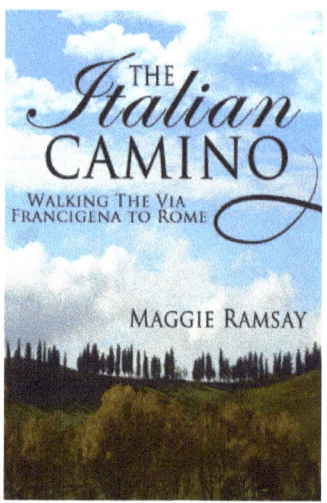

Walking from France to Rome might not sound like something to laugh about, but this book is funny. It is also full of great descriptions of the Swiss Alps, Tuscany and Rome, with side trips to Florence, Venice and Ravenna. The people along the way, the art, the history, the food—what's not to love? Walking for two months along an ancient pilgrimage route, mostly through forests and along back roads, makes for a very different travel experience.

Praise for The Italian Camino:
"I am married to an Italian and my children's father is Italian. I have always wanted to visit Italy, Switzerland and France. This story reads as such, a good story. An easy read, with lots of humor along with beautiful descriptions of the country this Australian couple walked through. Lots of interesting history and wonderful descriptions of appealing and not so appealing people that they met along the way. I loved reading about the meals they had and where they ate them. This was a quick and fun read." Frank. 5 Stars. Reviewed on August 15, 2013. Verified purchase.

My Camino in France

Take a walk through the South of France. A six-week walk, in fact, following a medieval pilgrimage trail, part of the world-famous Camino de Santiago. Four Australians set out from Le-Puy-en-Velay, heading for Spain. The path, through some of the most beautiful villages in France, is a feast of spectacular scenery and breathtaking architecture. Of course, walking off the beaten track and in all weathers makes for a truckload of funny, fascinating and unexpected encounters. Every day brings experiences that ricochet from the sublime to the ridiculous. It is immensely entertaining, endlessly interesting.

Praise for My Camino in France:
"Great read. Fun, inspiring and helpful. I'd recommend this book to anyone thinking of walking the Camino from Le Puy. It's very readable, with just the right amount of information and personal details." David John Cutler. 5 Stars. Reviewed on 22 August, 2017. Verified Purchase

www.ingramcontent.com/pod-product-compliance
Lightning Source LLC
Chambersburg PA
CBHW051538010526
44107CB00064B/2767